Presidential -
Maneuvering or Sandbagging?

The Battle Over Obamacare
In the Midst of a Debt Crisis –

A Politically Independent Perspective

TAEGER GILMIGHEL

MAC' ETHE

ISBN-10:1495490823
ISBN-13:9781495490828

DEDICATION

*To all reasonable thinking Americans
who want the U.S. government to stop
dictating political initiatives that are costing our
people and this country our freedoms.*

*The entire world is paying attention
to whether we are going to pay our debts,
setup new budgets or
let our debts spiral out of control.*

*I for one believe in the USA
and I believe we can rise above
these challenges and fix what is
ailing our great nation.*

*Let us each stand up
and make our voices heard.
Raise a political yell
for the brave and the free.*

CONTENTS

ACKNOWLEDGMENTS

The goal in writing this document is to relate an independent perspective or opinion you may not be aware of during the twilight of President Obama's Administration in the Whitehouse. Looking at the Battle over Obamacare in the midst of the largest debt crisis the United States of America has ever seen. These serious issues need to be seen from another side or perspective. Why is this serious?

It is important that the American people will not just listen to their local news or hear someone's opinion from the local radio. This is necessary in order to make sense of why President Obama has used his leadership to create a health care bill that is 2,572 pages long. It was initially created to help the under-served in America but it has backfired. This was created but at what price?

President Obama's advisors had probably mentioned to him that the only way to pay for these programs and bail out the American debt was to put everyone in America on the ACA, Obamacare or the Un-affordable Care Act. The problem with this strategy is this is a country that prides itself on being a land of volunteers. Our rights to volunteer for the President's health care plan cannot be realized due to the nature of the ACA Law.

President Obama must have realized that he wanted to make a difference and create a legacy but he gave no thought that he might have to kick his own Party members in the Senate and the House under the bus. In order to get his own remake of the Bill and Hillary Clinton National Health Care plan in motion he had to push the Democratic Party elite to force their own Party Democrats to go along even though they had no idea what was actually written into the law.

I can only speculate as to why President Obama's inner advisors or what I like to call his invisible counsel did not notify him that trying to provide anyone who works 30 hours or more benefits and insurance was not going to work and will actually hurt the people who voted for President Barack Obama into office. All across the United States of America all hourly workers have now been told their hours are being cut to 28 from 40 a week and now they can't afford to pay their bills, their mortgages, their car payments or food.

It is unfortunate that the presidency of Barack Obama is unaware that this has been tried before when contractors who worked for Microsoft sued them in court during the mid-1990's for benefits and insurance. The President of the United States of America has had the fight of his political life over the issues of Obamacare or the Un-affordable Care Act, Clean Continuing Resolution, Sequestration, the Debt Ceiling and Defaulting on our Sovereign debt are only a few of the problems many other problems that will not be easily fixed. To top it all off the President of the United States wants to force every American off their already existing decent health care plans, he also wants to force everyone to take the same health care plan.

The Democratic Party is digging in and fighting on one side while the Republican Party is fighting just as hard to stop their opponents on the other side of the aisle from gaining ground and laying these programs on the shoulders of the American People. One problem that Obamacare is not fixing is that it is not just the premiums of the insurance that the American people will have to pay for it is also that these new insurance packages will not pay for any elaborate medical needs a person may have in the future.

What is interesting is that President Obama has every intention of following through with the 20 new taxes that have been created just to supplement Obamacare which will kick in on January 2014. He has added more than a billion dollar's worth of interest groups that he wants to fund before his presidency ends. These were not created to assist anyone or anything as noble as helping the American people. These new interest groups were supposedly created to pay back those who supported his bid for the Whitehouse.

If a person needs to see their doctor presently they have to wait 33 days but under Obamacare the same people who are already waiting 33 days will have to wait 55 days to see their doctors. This is an unacceptable mandate and unnecessary stipulation of Obamacare. Any person who has a health care need can and should see their physician whenever they feel the need to do it. This is why we pay health care and medical insurance. If we are not allowed to see our doctor after paying medical insurance than why should we keep any particular medical coverage. The Democrats in the House and Senate are going to switch sides and vote with the GOP to fix these issues with Obamacare before their own constituents turn against them in the next election.

How can President Obama stick to his guns while he has been informed that his own political party is bailing from President Obama's plan to fleece the middle class with his new vision for medical coverage? Even Representative Pelosi is continuing to stick to her guns even though many of the Democrats are no longer supporting President Obama.

The Democratic elite of Senator Harry Reid and Representative Pelosi can no longer control the Democratic party now that they are scrambling to save their own political careers. If any of the Democrats are serious about wanting to be re-elected they will not only bail from Obamacare but they will cross party lines to vote with House and Senate Republicans to repeal or rewrite the ACA to fix all mandates back to voluntary.

These vast changes over Obamacare, the debt ceiling, sequestration, the default over debts and the course of the U.S. Government shutdown of October 1st, 2013 have brought attention to President Obama's lack of understanding as to how the American people will react to their freedoms being diminished. Everyone in the Democratic Party as well as the Republican Party have used brinkmanship to increase their popularity and continue their efforts in Washington, D.C. What has not been obvious until now is that President Obama thought that Bill and Hillary Clinton's ideas of National Health care which Hillary created during former President Bill Clinton's Administration was a great way to solidify his own legacy and continue to increase big government to the next level.

Strategically President Obama miss-calculated how the people would react after they realized they had been duped. Even his strongest supporters are recognizing that he had no intention of following through with his promises. The American people are starting to realize that the President of the United States of America already knew that

Obamacare was not going to work but he went through with it anyway knowing it was going to fail. This is a breach of trust with the American people and there is only so much trust that will be offered by the news media who normally stand by the president.

When the ballast has been lost and the ship is no longer worthy to set sail the media will dump their support and they will speak about the Tea Party as those who believe in democracy, as those who believe in freedom of religion, as those who believe in free speech, as those who believe in free enterprise...these are what made the United States of America a very special place and the most powerful nation on earth.

The American people see that the Republicans have been trying to resolve U. S. problems with our debt and will now try to use the failures of Obamacare, to present different alternatives and opportunities to flip the sequestration, debt ceiling and diminish government intervention into the lives of ordinary Americans citizens by defunding the Un-affordable Care Act. This is really dependent upon whether the Democrats in the Senate and the House are willing to negotiate and bring attention to their willingness to compromise which may be able to protect their political careers during the next election.

1 INTRODUCTION

This is a political perspective concerning presidential maneuvering and sandbagging on the part of President Obama, the Republican Party leadership in the U.S. House of Representatives and the Democratic Party within the U.S. Senate. The Republican Party in the House were trying to sandbag the President of the United States into giving more ground on political initiatives before the U.S. economy tanked and we defaulted on our sovereign debt.

The problem with this kind of bantering and competitiveness is moot if the other side knows you have no intention of following through with your promises. President Obama knew that Republican leadership and Tea Party radicals in the House of Representatives had no intention of defaulting on our country's sovereign debt so he continued to stall right up until the last day of the default.

The Republican Party on many occasions has worked with President Obama and the Democratic leadership in the Senate to resolve issues. During the last four and a half years the Republican leadership were pretty sure they understood what was important to President Obama but they failed to recognize that he had reached his point of no return on September 2013. He was not going to budge any further on the ACA or Affordable Care Act.

It has been shared in the House and the Senate that President Obama had changed the wording on the ACA law several times in the Summer of 2013 to de-fund parts of Obamacare which had too much funding but when the President realized the Republican Party leadership in the House were going to go after the ACA he felt pushed into a corner.

If he let down his guard during the Call For Conference President Obama would have felt that he had been bullied. He had no intention of letting the Republicans change any part of the ACA until he was positive it would ultimately be left alone. The President was not going to show signs of weakness in his second term in the Whitehouse. I personally believe that

1

all our political leaders have the best interests of America at heart.

Each political party and each leader at the local, regional, state and national levels want to make a difference and serve the American people with honor. They have taken up the reigns of leadership and are trying their level best to make sense of these issues as they work tirelessly across both sides of the aisle to work together for the benefit of all the people of the United States of America.

It is important to each of us at some point in our lives when we all find ourselves wanting to make a significant contribution in our efforts to be men and women of integrity. Sometimes we do this because we are trying to reach out to those within our circle of influence whether they are at work, our colleagues, our friends or our family. All of us at times lose sight of what is important. The only difference is how we go about making the correct decisions as we work to fix important issues that will affect our family, friends and neighbors.

In order for all of us in America to treat one another properly we need to be open minded. We need to be trustworthy and we need to trust those of different political parties so they can trust us and know that we are going to do our best too. We need to realize that these political issues must be addressed. This book was written to bring attention to the ideals of which the United States of America was founded.

We all feel that life, liberty, and the pursuit of happiness is a pretty good thing and a great ideal and we agree that we need to work together to solve the issues that plague this great nation. We can no longer sit back on our laurels and think any of these problems are going to go away.

We need to be just as determined to solve the problems as we are to work together to resolve these issues at the national level. Some of the leaders of the Senate and the House have been known to go about mud-slinging or referring to one another as a terrorist or an anarchist. This is part of being tough competitors and wanting one political party to get one over on the other party. This is also called playing hardball, or trash-talking to try to get a rise out of another competitor.

I truly believe that President Obama has worked very hard to create solutions that will drive change in this country for everyone's benefit. All presidents have political, economic, foreign policy, situational, conflict, international, and domestic advisors that they rely on to give them the big picture as to what should be done, what will be the effects of change and what kind of fallout may ensue regarding these outcomes during different problematic situations. The responsibilities of the President of the United States is to strengthen the U.S. economy, provide solutions that will honor and protect the people of the United States.

Each presidency has an organizational breakdown of how they keep information flowing within the hierarchy in order to affect change and

2

influence domestic and international relations. One of the items on the President's domestic agenda is his legacy which is a fulcrum to effect change in the health care of those who have never been served and provide avenues for affordable care to everyone who needs it.

He also sees the need to keep this country intact for future generations by creating programs that will protect the fiscal solvency, the people, the political, the economic and the military strength of America. You cannot create your legacy alone and if the most powerful person in the world continues to sandbag moderates in the Senate and the House he will find himself unsupported by his own party.

The Democrats and the Republican Party moderates in both the House and the Senate who were willing to work in a bi-partisan manner in order to affect change and make the ACA work is commendable. Before anyone starts to blame the President it is important to note that he was not alone in creating the 2,572 pages of the law.

2 WHOSE IDEA WAS THE ACA ?

This idea of the ACA was the brain child introduced during former President Bill Clinton's Administrations by he and his wife Hillary Clinton who championed the goal of helping all people and wanted to make health care coverage affordable. Due to several issues and problems trying to set this in motion during former President Bill Clinton's Administration the broad strokes of creating an Affordable Care Act for the under-served needed to be tabled till a later date when these problems could be hammered out.

I personally believe that Hillary would have done her best to work with both sides of the aisle to make a National Health Care plan that was not going to fleece American pocketbooks. No small wonder why former Secretary of State Hillary Clinton resigned during President Obama's Administration. She knew that the Affordable Care Act created under President Obama had serious problems and she was not in any way responsible for the malignant manner in which it was being implemented. Once it became the law of the land she knew there was going to be fallout and she needed to step away from being implicated in its demise.

She along with many members of the Democratic Party elite knew that this was going to create many problems on both sides of the aisles. Hillary Clinton needed to distance herself from the Affordable Care Act to avoid any of the anticipated problems prior to its implementation. She also did not want these mandates to affect her bid to run for Presidential office.

Hillary Clinton along with the Democratic Leadership elite evangelists in the Senate knew that to make this bill a reality several Democrats would have to put their own political careers on the line to push this new bill into law. To make sure the Democrats in the U.S. Senate towed the line Senator Harry Reid of Nevada had to put a strangle-hold on several Democrats or kick them under the bus of change to get the vote completed on the ACA.

Former Secretary of State Hillary Rodham Clinton was more than willing to speak out about the needs of the under-served when her husband was the President of the United States. What is interesting is that Bill Clinton's advisors during his Administration were smart enough to avoid trying to create this bill while he was in office. They knew after speaking to their advisors and crunching the numbers that the only way to fund such a program was to place an undue burden on the middle-class that voted them into office by adding several taxes.

Former Secretary of State Hillary Clinton resigned in the middle of President Obama's presidency because she needed to walk away from the Obama Administration and the Obamacare knowing she was one of the initial architects of this idea during former President Bill Clinton's Administration. It should be called Clintoncare considering this was her and her husband's brainchild. It was either her advisors or former President Bill Clinton's who shared with her that she cannot afford to be anywhere near the fallout of Obamacare in order to start preparing for her own bid to run for President of the United States and the Whitehouse.

If you have been watching the news you will notice that the former Secretary of State has been out of the lime light for some time. In previous years Hillary Rodham Clinton was always willing to talk with both sides of the aisle and was known for being willing to work in bi-partisan politics to seek win-win solutions. When she first got involved in politics after finishing her law degree she was a Republican. She later changed her mind as she became a spokesperson for the under-served.

During these last several months she has kept a very low profile and is not speaking to the media on any topics so she can keep her political career in check until the next election. This will give her full deniability when she announces her candidacy to the media in front of the national spotlight. There are two reasons why Hillary Clinton would hold back from speaking out in support of the Obama Administration during the implementation of the Affordable Care Act.

The first reason is due to her need to avoid any problems as she steps into the political arena and starts her campaign to run for President of the United States. She cannot afford any tenuous connections to President Obama and any of the present administration's failure to solve the issues with this 2,572 page fiasco.

The second reason has to do with her idea to initially bring up the need for a National Health care plan when she was outspoken under former President Bill Clinton's Administration. This is something she was very adamant about and wanted to setup for those that were being under served. Now that it is a law Hillary Rodham Clinton knows that President Obama will be blamed for most of the problems even though he was not the person who was the initial architect and came up with the idea in the first place.

In looking over these issues from a politically independent perspective it is not a stretch of the imagination to deduce that former Secretary of State Hillary Clinton was very much involved in the initial planning of the Affordable Care Act. She shared her concerns and ideas to President Obama and the president's advisors must have shared with the President that this is a great legacy to pass on to future generations and would solidify his place in history. President Obama had Senator Reid and Representative Pelosi making sure the rest of the Democratic Party in the Senate and the House towed the line, stayed focused and silent.

During the 17 day stand-off it was rare to see any Democrats in the Senate or the House walking to the podium to share the needs of their constituents. We heard from only a few Democrats like Senator Al Franken speaking about what Minnesota's people were dealing with as their hourly workers had the hours cut the moment companies started to realize they needed to cut the hours back below 30 hours to avoid paying benefits and insurance to their hourly workers.

The Un-affordable Care Act or the wording of Obamacare identified that anyone who has 30 or more hours a week are entitled to benefits and insurance. The problem is that every hourly employee who had 40+ hours per week prior to the implementation of Obamacare is having their hours cut to 28 hours per week instead of the usual 40. How does this affect Joe the plumber, the person President Barack Obama was speaking with during the campaign for his presidency? Joe will not be able to work his full time job any longer since his hours will be cut from 40 to 28 hours per week and now he will be considered part-time.

How many hours will employees lose over the course of a month if they were hourly employees and dropped from 40 to 28 hours. They will lose 12 per week and 48 hours per month. In a year this will be equal to almost 1/3rd of their pay or 600 hours lost permanently from their annual income. President Obama promised the American people that their insurance would not be cut, they would not lose their doctors and their pay would not be affected.

President Obama's Press Secretary stated that only 5% of American workers would be affected by these changes. If they were remotely accurate they could be talking about 16 million people losing one third of their pay. Is this 5% of American workers who voted for President Obama considered acceptable losses? Let us not talk in percentages of people but in hard numbers.

The Federal government is notorious for underestimating what this will cost the American people. At least 10% of the United States has now lost one third of their pay per year and that equals a minimum of 32.5 million people. How many people have to lose a third of their pay before the people will start picketing in the streets of Washington, DC?

When will the Democrats in the House and the Senate step up and start fighting for the rights of their constituents to get their pay returned to them? When will the Democrats and the Republicans demand to return the hours of hardworking Americans back to them so they can pay for their mortgages, their clothes and to put food on their tables? This administration should never have placed a mandate on businesses to give their hourly employees benefits and insurance.

If Mitt Romney had won the presidency or if someone like Representative John Boehner became president of the United States they would never have placed hourly employees under the bus the way this administration has done. Why not? The reason Representative John Boehner or Mitt Romney would not have added the hourly workers to the ACA if they had created such a bill is because both of these men started as businessmen. They know what would ensue had they added hourly workers to the law. They know as businessmen that hourly workers would simply have their hours cut by their employers or their jobs would have been eliminated.

This is what businesses do. They find the silver lining in all the present circumstances and save on their bottom-line to keep their business solvent. It is good business to find what works and continue to do it in business. This should never have been put into the Obamacare package. When will the Democrats and the Republicans start to speak out for the rights of the American people and say they are no longer going to wait for the President and his staff to straighten it out? They need to submit bills to repeal, defund and eliminate it. Obamacare has to be paid for and the Federal Government is going to pay for it by adding 20 new taxes on January 1st, 2014 to pay for the Un-affordable Care Act.

One would think it is obvious that the American people who work hourly jobs will need to continue to work full time and at 40 hours a week or more to be able to pay these outrageous taxes to pay for insurance we do not need and can't afford. We need to have the wording within the 2,572 pages of the Un-Affordable Care Act to read that it is entirely voluntary. It also needs wording within the ACA that any hourly workers who works more than 60 hours per week should be given full benefits and insurance.

Former Secretary of State Hillary Rodham Clinton is going to run for a bid to become the President of the United States. She is going to say during her campaign that she will work to fix the Affordable Care Act. She will use many points to identify that she has worked on many occasions on both sides of the aisle to work together with her counterparts. If people believe what she says and vote her into office she will make very small changes to the Un-affordable Care Act. It will not be in her best interests to   make any sweeping changes that will affect her plans to increase government spending. No matter what her promises will be towards fixing Obamacare it will go on deaf ears when she speaks to the American people unless she were to stand up before announcing her presidency to say it was handled incorrectly which she will not do. What is interesting is that Hillary Rodham Clinton's husband former President Bill Clinton did make an announcement to the media stating that whatever promises were made to the American people by President Barack Obama needs to be given to the people, the President of the United States must fulfill his promises.

President Obama is a very intelligent leader and we need to realize that he may have been ill advised by several within his inner circle or invisible counsel of advisors. His closest advisors may only talk to him concerning possible scenarios that might play out elsewhere. I would say that most presidents are advised to stay clear of controversy that might ensue so they can have and claim full deniability if any problems arise during their presidency which may find them in a position in which they inadvertently broke the law.

It is these close connections with their multiple advisors that help Presidents protect themselves from onslaughts which may create unwanted fallout while carrying out unethical tasks. Every president has close advisors who give them counsel and protect their integrity with allies. I feel President Obama probably has several advisors which I like to call his invisible counsel which we never see but we know exists.

His advisors who see the big picture and are willing to give him only the meat of the problem so they can protect him. Some U.S. President's have been engaged at the very highest level of command and have found themselves in a fire storm in which they could not recover politically and it most likely cost them their 2nd term in the Whitehouse.

Other U.S. Presidents setup several layers of advisors in order to have their people making sure the President of the United States is given some but not all the information. I believe that it is this type of advising that has been setup to protect President Obama but may have cost him his legacy in the long run due to him not knowing the wording of the Affordable Care Act.

Of course it is very presidential to protect the Commander in Chief if there are looming issues that he has no control over in order to shield him from any onslaughts but this is not one of those times. President Obama promised to have an open discussion concerning the Affordable Care Act. The President also said we would have bi-partisan support and then pushed it through without letting the Republican Party share in the debate, development and creation of the bill. This is not only wrong but may have called the President's leadership into question concerning flawed decision-making principals. Speaking to those who are waiting for you to follow through with your requests for the Call for Conference and then refusing to negotiate reeks of coercive diplomacy and a lack of conflict management.

This is actually a method by which President Obama was setting up the Republicans in the House to fail at negotiating. Passing a law which Washington D.C. and the Democrats in the Senate are demanding people to follow blindly is actually considered a manipulative threat to collaborative efforts. This could be considered a strange ploy or strategy to garner more sympathy for the Democratic Party. When we consider that the President has been advised by several layers of advisors to ignore the Republicans after promising they would have enough time to meet in conference seems odd.

Refusing to meet with Republicans in conference makes President Obama seem irresponsible. There are strategic behaviors used in diplomacy with international states that I believe President Obama was using to control Republican leaders in the House during the 2013 Government shutdown. This is a real strategy called coercive diplomacy. President Obama used it to demand only one option from Republican leaders in the House and by initiating this method he was giving no other manner in which to communicate.

Passing Obamacare in the Senate without a single Republican vote and without any debate or open discussion from the House of Representatives seems ill advised since it closes the door to bi-partisan discussions. Meeting for the Call for Conference means that the President of the United States requested the Republican Leadership to go to the Whitehouse to come to speak about the issues. It sounds like a simple request but it is often used as a way to demand a meeting and when you are called by the President of the United States of America it is not a request, you must go to see the president in the Whitehouse.

My goal in sharing my independent perspective is to be honest concerning what was happening during the government shutdown and what transpired between the President, the Republican Party and the Democratic Party. I am not attempting to sugar-coat my perspective. The truth is often against popular opinion, which is why so many prefer to avoid it.

As an independent perspective it is hard to avoid the obvious. We all remember the promises made and broken by President Obama when he stated emphatically that if you liked your doctor and your health care plan you would be allowed to keep them. Amazingly President Obama has not tried to drop his promises but has been trying to keep the promises he gave to the American people. Just because the ACA is a law does not mean it cannot be changed, reworded or fixed to straighten out these very real problems from further affecting the American people.

If President Obama works to fix these issues for the American people by completely overhauling the 2,572 pages of the ACA and lifts these mandates to the American people and not just the employers than his legacy may not be destroyed. The ACA needs to be rewritten and not necessarily thrown out by the President and his Party if they are going to save face politically. If they do not take the initiative to fix it then the Republican Party will create bills to straighten out Obamacare and make all its' policies and mandates voluntary.

If the Republican Party creates a new bill repealing Obamacare and the Senate agrees in its bi-partisan support than two things will happen. The first thing the Democrats in the House and the Senate will do is cross the aisle so they will keep their jobs and be voted back into office since they took the necessary steps to protect the American people. The second thing the Republican Party will win the next election and will work to reverse every decision that President Obama created while in office and at the same time will work to strengthen the economy, balance the budget, eliminate sequestration and pay back our Sovereign debt.

If the American people want to increase their net worth, protect their way of life and move the ACA to become voluntary, they will be voting the next Republican into the Whitehouse with a land slide victory. Strictly speaking from my independent perspective there are many candidates that could easily run for the Whitehouse from the Republican side. I personally think one man in particular is a voice of reason and has been a businessman since he first entered office in the House of Representatives.

They would make an excellent candidate and everyone knows that we need someone in office that understands the process. We need someone in office that gets what the American people are feeling and we cannot afford the U.S. Government to continue to get larger and pay all these taxes we are about to be levied against us. If for no other reason than the American people cannot afford 20 more taxes to fund a healthcare plan that was a failure the day it was enacted. It cannot remain a law unless major revisions are made and soon.

The Republican Party will also be doing something else that most Americans are not aware of and are usually oblivious to regarding the protection of the United States of America and its borders. Most Veterans already understand that if we are not fighting our enemies overseas we could find ourselves fighting them in our streets.

Sequestration has got to be one of the most irresponsible mandates placed on our military. We need to remove critical responsibilities such as the Power Grid and Military Logistics from being mishandled under sequestration.

It took till November 2013 for President Obama to get on the National spotlight and tell the American people he was sorry that some people did not get to keep their insurance after he promised they could. Some people? The American people have already realized that Obamacare failed and all of these initiatives need to stop right now!

Too little, too late! President Obama needs to be smart enough to know that his ratings will increase if he takes more ownership and fixes these necessary rewrites or shuts down the Obamacare. It is worth something when you see a Commander in Chief who is willing to apologize for breaking his promise to the American people.

The American people respond to actions not words. The people want to know that the ACA is voluntary only or completely shut down. They want to know that they will not have to lose one third their pay annually, they want to know that the economy is going to grow. The President of the United States is going to fix these issues in the next six months or the people will be calling for a resignation.

Our President is trying to stand up to the scrutiny and be willing to tell people he will do his best to keep his promises. We however do not have such a president. He did not even show up in the media to apologize until it was obvious that Obamacare was seriously failing. It took former President Bill Clinton to step into the spotlight and state that the President of the United States made promises he will need to honor to the American people.

This is not enough, the American people already know that they are flipping the bill on these out of focus programs and whoever is running the U.S. Government is going to force all of us to pay for Obamacare, Sequestration, and the Debt Ceiling. Most Americans are going to get a rude awakening when they realize that the Federal Government is going to pay for the Un-affordable Care Act with more taxes which will be levied on the American people starting on January 1st, 2014.

Around that same time large price reduced stores are laying off workers or they are cutting their hours back in order to avoid having to pay their workers any insurance or benefits. What would make the people want to vote another Democrat back into the Whitehouse knowing that it will only be more of the same rhetoric.

How many more taxes is the next Democrat in the Whitehouse going to levy upon the American people? Will we continue to lose more freedoms and the U.S. Government continues to get larger? The United States of America really has serious issues that need to be addressed. The American people must be rather naive if they do not think that President Obama has forcefully crossed the line and has weakened this country for his own agenda. What am I saying to you?

I am saying that President Obama has turned his back on our allies and Israel. He has been negotiating with the president of Iran, the president of Syria and the Taliban. The president of Iran kowtows to Iran's Supreme religious leader. The president of Iran is presenting himself to the world as a moderate but he is light years from the lamb he makes himself out to be. This is not difficult to understand, our president has never served in the military. He has no idea what it takes to defend a nation.

There is a law within the Koran that states that if you feel you need to lie to take advantage of your enemies and protect your religious beliefs you are allowed to lie. Why did President Obama speak with and say he was willing to negotiate with Terrorist Nation States such as Iran, Syria and the Taliban? These Terrorist leaders openly share their hatred for Americans. They have not changed their tack or their willingness to attack us here in the United States and cause great fear in the hearts of the infidels as they call us. If we do not back ourselves out of this situation with Iran we will find ourselves causing conflicts and wars they will start now that sanctions are lifting. This is the path their supreme religious leader has chosen for them to hate Americans and their allies. What do we gain in opening lines of communication with Iran, Syria and the Taliban?

According to our military leaders in Afghanistan our soldiers are only allowed to stop our enemies from killing one another. If our soldiers see a person beating his wife in Afghanistan we are not allowed to intervene with their beliefs or domestic agenda. We are only in those countries to assist as military trainers. If we see any inhumane violations we are not allowed to intervene. If our soldiers see anything that we feel is unacceptable and against human rights we are under orders to avoid it and just let it go.

President Barack Obama is not the problem here but he understands exactly what our middle east neighbors believe and why they are wanting to keep their inert nuclear program in place. They are willing to negotiate in order to get the sanctions dropped that have crippled their nation and once they have the sanctions lifted and their 4 billion dollars returned to them they will increase their efforts to enrich uranium and plutonium for the production of weapons of mass destruction. We have responsibilities not only to Israel but to our allies and the free world that we will protect their rights as well.

When we begin to look at this new ACA law we need to take a moment to ask some questions that might shed light on these serious issues. How much money did President Obama save the American people during his first term in office? In his first term in office President Obama and Ben Bernanke were bailing out the banks that were too big to fail. The new President of the United States, President Obama had inherited the problems of former President George W. Bush Jr. from the huge debts that were mounting up from the war in Iraq and Afghanistan to the failing of the markets and the banks.

These issues were not created by President Obama but he knew that if he was going to make his own legacy a reality he would have to take on the huge debts caused by the war and the bank bailouts. President Obama needed Mr. Bernanke to assist his Administration so the economy would look like it was rebounding even though printing billions to pay our debts creates the opposite effect.

Now that President Obama is in his second term he is working to make his legacy a reality with Obamacare, Sequestration, the Debt Ceiling and the Sovereign Debt. How does he plan to pay for all of this? The two ways to fix the United States of America in a financial crisis is difficult. It will have to be either he is going to raise taxes or he will cut programs. We know that President Obama did both.

I do not remember getting any tax breaks but I believe he held back in giving us more taxes. In his first term in office. We know that the President was working with Democratic lawmakers to put together a plan in which the people who had not been covered previously in health care would be in the very near future.

His promises of saving the American people $2500 on their coverage is not possible with 17 trillion owed. A blanket statement telling everyone they would save on their coverage is a statistical impossibility. Most people in America knew that the president would not be able to help everyone but most of us did not expect that we would be told we had no choice. This is a country of volunteers, you cannot expect people to go along with a mandate when one is not needed.

Not only are these promises unrealistic but the basic insurance package will cost the average family $20,000 a year in deductibles. This is only the tip of the iceberg. What I mean by the tip of the iceberg is that if the government built a brand new health care and insurance plan for the entire country who do you think is going to pay for it?

This is not brain surgery, it doesn't take a mathematician to calculate who will have to pay for this program. The country owes 17 trillion dollars to other countries so we already know this country cannot afford to spend money we do not have on programs that will not work. The Democrats built this monster cash cow and now they want all of us to flip the bill. Guess what?

The federal government has given another $500 million dollars to the IRS in anticipation of fining those who refuse to pay the 20 new tax bills that will be charged to everyone to make sure they are prepared for the next little surprise we will see starting in January 1st, 2014. Our president is going to pass bills in the Senate to add 20 more new tax hikes to pay for Obamacare. This is totally unacceptable.

How much money are Americans going to be able to save if they are paying 20 new tax hikes starting in January 2014 on top of the taxes we are already paying and with one third less pay? The answer is simple...nothing. How many promises need to be given and broken and lies given before the American people will demand that their Congressman and Senators start proceedings to impeach the President of the United States? How many people have signed up for Obamacare out of the 350,000,000 +/- people in this country? Less than 1/100th of 1% have quite literally sign up online.

This is why the president and his invisible counsel of advisors have cooked up this plan and convinced the Supreme Court that everyone should have the right to have health insurance. Not because they want to help the American people, once the Supreme Court accepted the brief as it was presented the Democrats and the President of the United States knew that Obamacare was going to become a law. Once President Obama had the Supreme Court's support he was going to take the earliest opportunity to have the ACA voted into law before the Republicans in the House could stop it. Not because it is important for the people but because it bails out the Democrats in the Senate, U.S. Debt, the economy and sequestration. It is imperative to get this country back on its feet but at what price? Making all of us join Obamacare in order to sell these plans to us blindly.

We need real answers to real problems. Adding 20 new taxes to the American people will not fix the problems. We need to grow the economy. It cannot be done on the back of the middle class, it must be done by increasing opportunities for new businesses and providing discounts to existing medical coverage like Medicare and Medicaid.

The Democratic Party needs to continue to make the American people pay for bigger government. Why? The vision of the Democratic Party is to increase government and charge more taxes to pay for all the programs and initiatives created to help the American people despite the fact that the people will be paying for all these programs we do not want and do not need. What is the best and easiest way to increase the size of government? Add more taxes to the American people to fund all these ludicrous ideas that no one can afford.

Why would anyone listen to the Democratic Representative of California Nancy Pelosi when she said on National TV "No one knows what's inside the new Affordable Care Act, let's just vote on it and then we will see what's in it." That is the craziest line I ever heard from an elected official. How can an elected official sell out their responsibilities to their constituents? The very same American people they vowed to protect once they were in office.

That is the most ridiculous statement I have ever heard. If anyone said that line while working for any company in America they would have been fired that day. The truth is far more complex due to the wording of bills and laws before they are passed by the Senate and the House of Representatives. The bills must be written in such a manner that the wording follows specific boilerplates used in the Senate and the House of Representatives.

Due to the wording of these documents they are not easily read by legislative officials which is why Democratic Representative Nancy Pelosi stated that the Senate needed to go ahead and vote on it. The ACA law is 2,572 pages long and we know that President Barack Obama has not read the Affordable Care Act. No Senators or Congressman from the house have had the time to read it. It still holds true that the vote should never have taken place in the Senate. It is absolutely wrong to have people vote on any bill unless you completely understand the wording of that bill. Representative Pelosi was just echoing what most people in Washington, D.C. already know about the ACA law.

Unless the American people are asleep they are going to show up in droves to vote these 16 Democratic Senate leaders who helped create Obamacare out of office along with Senator Harry Reid and Representative Nancy Pelosi for going along with adding 20 new taxes to the American people to pay for a health care plan that has already failed and they continue to shove down our throats.

How is it that the media didn't jump on this quote from Rep. Pelosi? Telling Senate leadership to vote on it and then look at what's in the law has got to be an act of lunacy. Why didn't the media question her? Is it because many of these TV News Stations agree with Democratic hardliners? Maybe the political agenda of the media is in line with adding scores of taxes to the American people to fund a health care plan that no one can afford?

We can remember the promises made to the American people during the campaign from both parties as each ran for another term in the House or the Senate. Some members of both parties took on the entrenched incumbents trying to show their Party and their constituents that change was necessary. Some of the incumbents lost their support and elections while others succeeded in their attempts.

This is why Democracy works in America. We have all seen many different kinds of political maneuvering and it is nothing new. This is not the only way to get things passed in the Senate or the House. Sometimes people who are considered Democratic or Republican Party leadership can influence a select number of members. This is done when it is necessary to hold back others who would normally be willing to cross Party lines to the other side of the aisle and work for bi-partisan solutions to issues that cannot be fixed without compromise from both parties.

Sometimes the media will call this maneuvering "creating a spin," in order to change or redirect influence within a political party or to bring attention to something that has not been called into question. At the same time there is maneuvering either from within all parties and amongst the same party to go in a particular direction when influenced or manipulated to do it. These can create additional complexities to influence individuals or groups within several distinct alternative political views. We can only speculate as to why President Obama felt he had been backed into a corner or was put into a position that forced him to refuse further negotiations. It seemed clear that his advisors directed him to start stonewalling the

Republican Party on these topics using international coercive diplomacy.

Refusing all communication when backed into a corner may have left President Obama without a lot of avenues to break the gridlock or stalemate.

What is interesting to me is that Republican Party leadership could not communicate any further once President Obama stopped negotiating. The House continued to pass incremental bills in order to keep the government open but each time they sent the bills to the floor of the Senate they were rejected. President Obama might have felt he had been forced into a corner but he was not dissuaded from continuing his duties as President of the United States of America. He still had duties to perform and he may have seemed down but he was never out.

As an independent I would have to say that the only voice of reason I was hearing during the time of the government shutdown was coming from the Republican camp with Representative John Boehner. President Obama had nothing on his agenda dealing with NATO allies and he wanted to shake up the Republican Party in particular to get them to release the Clean Continuing Resolution so he could continue to fund Obamacare. The government was shut down but this opened up time for President Obama to open up discussions with Iran, Syria and the Taliban.

Why would the leader of the free world open communication with those countries that hate us most unless this is on his international agenda and part of his presidential legacy. Looking from a purely independent perspective the move to open communications with Iran, Syria and the Taliban gave avenues for the President of Iran to stop the sanctions on his country and get the billions of dollars that were seized by United States officials back to Iran.

Any move towards communicating with Iran's new President would be seen as positive and could create another notch in President Obama's international legacy. A win-win for the Democratic Party to show the world that we are willing to open up negotiations for international diplomacy.

3 MANEUVERING OR SANDBAGGING ?

If the Republican Party leadership and their advisors felt that sandbagging was the only way in which to get President Obama's attention to these very serious problems then I believe you got his attention. In a seemingly normal manner each incremental bill passed in the House was that much more infuriating to President Obama since it simply and very slowly opened the government but did not open the discussion for the Clean CR which President Obama demanded before he would negotiate on any other policy or legislation.

In this sense President Obama was maneuvering himself into a position that the Republican Party leadership would also see as sandbagging since they were not able to communicate unless they were willing to place their one bargaining chip the Clean CR onto the table before the president would open any other discussions. Looking at this from both the House and the Senate it seems clear that the Republicans in the House were using the Clean CR to stop President Obama from moving forward with the ACA, Sequestration, the Debt Ceiling and Defaulting on our Sovereign debt.

If for no other reason than to just get the President to look at how these problems were going to send our country over the fiscal cliffs and into the global debt abyss. The U.S. Senate felt that holding the Clean CR or Continuing Resolution from President Obama was going to cause all of his worst fears to come true. If the Republicans were going to hold the Clean CR and not give it to the President of the United States than how will the President be able to move forward with the debt looming, the sequestration or to have open talks concerning the ACA or the debt ceiling?

The President clearly stated several times that he was not willing to talk about the ACA, debt ceiling, defaulting on debt and sequestration until the Republicans gave up the Clean CR. The Republicans in the House were no longer interested in having those talks. Is it possible that the Clean CR was the very last bargaining chip Republicans in the House had at their disposal to stop the Democrats from going forward?

When the government first shutdown everyone wanted to blame each other but whose fault is it really? From an independent perspective it seemed like it was a fault of both sides since they were no longer communicating concerning any of these important issues. Watching Democratic and Republican Senators on the floor bickering, complaining and asking to get back to the issues of the day seemed quite relevant. When hearing the Republicans and Democrats in the House also started complaining, sharing and asking for their bi-partisan counterparts to get back to the House of Representatives this also seemed quite relevant.

What is not so relevant is who was controlling the Democratic Party and pulling their strings? President Obama was being protected by not only Democratic leadership in the Senate but by his advisors in his invisible counsel that keep him protected in the Whitehouse. How could President Obama be responsible for the actions of others who misinformed him of the mistakes in the wording of the ACA, Sequestration, Debt Ceiling and Sovereign debt? Was he really that naive, I don't think so.

President Barack Obama is no fool, he is clearly in command of his Presidency yet he was using International Diplomacy to force the hand of Republican leadership during the government shutdown. Clearly President Obama was using coercive diplomacy to rattle those in the Republican leadership and moderates within the Senate and House.

What is interesting is that either the Bilderberg Group or another world-wide global economic power group seemed to be pulling the strings. One can only speculate how far down the rabbit hole Alice had fallen since he had full deniability regarding the wording of the Un-Affordable Care Act. How far down the wrong path does the President have to go before he will realize that none of these programs were written the way he intended and he needs to get involved to straighten them out? During this same time President Obama was still able to continue his duties as President of the United States. He purposely opened lines of communication with terrorist political actors and nation states and onto any other platform including the world's stage to communicate with Iran, Syria and even the Taliban.

He continued his duties as the Commander in Chief while he was sandbagging the Republican Party over defaulting on the debt which was looming. He knew that he had to win and gain the Clean CR even for a little while. The Republican Party stated in the media several times that they were not going to default on the debt. They knew ultimately that they could not continue to stall and had to let go of their bargaining chip – the Clean CR and identify several offers in order to get President Obama to agree to a deal before the default.

In the end President Obama held out for his principles but at what cost? He gained a temporary Clean CR and did not lose Obamacare even though it is flawed and is going to cost this country more than 1.6 Trillion dollars to implement. It remains a complete failure. It is damaging families and destroying livelihoods now that hourly employees have had 48 hours cut each month and will probably be repealed unless the political parties do not understand that most Americans live paycheck to paycheck and needed to not have these 40 hours cut to below 30 hours.

The Un-Affordable Care Act states that anyone who works more than 30 hours per week is entitled to full benefits and insurance. What the wording did in the ACA was cause the people who voted for President Obama who were hourly to lose their jobs, or 48 hours a month in wages. Paying their utilities, mortgages, car payment bills are going to increase their suffering as they are forced to get another job.

Obamacare will certainly need to be fixed before it will work on the website as well as in Health and Human Services. The President of the United States has been sandbagging not just the Republican leadership in the House but also the Democrats in the Senate and in the House. President Obama wanted to implement Obamacare even though they already know that the Health and Human Services or HHS has not had enough time to fix the problems that already exist.

The problems with the HHS have been identified by the Office of Inspector Generals or OIG after auditing the 300 HHS programs and services in use across the United States of America. The OIG checked all possible vulnerabilities in each one of the 300 locations around the United States and verified that HHS needed to address each of the seven vulnerabilities which were not being fixed. The Health and Human Services wrote a plan identifying what they were going to do to fix those issues but before they could implement the plan President Obama wanted to go ahead and implement the Un-Affordable Care Act.

It seems logical that the Un-Affordable Care Act should not be implemented before the Health and Human Services fixes the problems in every facility of the 300 locations across the United States and setup proper protection for the technology and computers, the protection of Social Security Numbers, records and financial issues identified by the Office of Inspector Generals. It is unfortunate that President Obama is forcing the Un-Affordable Care Act to be implemented even though Health and Human Services is not ready for this implementation.

The HHS or Health and Human Services has been cited by the OIG or Office of Inspector Generals who are taxed with auditing the procedures and checking security risks and vulnerabilities. More than "Seven" systems have failed and the HHS hasn't implemented any fixes at this time. Health and Human Services has only written a report and a plan concerning how they need to fix it and about what they need to do to implement proper procedures to protect citizen's private data and social security numbers.

In his rush to push Obamacare on every citizen in the USA. President Obama is hurting not just the citizens who voted him in office he is damaging the political careers of the Democratic Party in particular. The Democrats will also be blamed when this law is fully implemented and fails to provide affordable care to millions of U. S. citizens. If I am wrong in my assessment of these hours why is it these huge discount vendors are stating that they will have to cut workers and the hours of thousands of others who have now lost one third their pay due to the wording written into the ACA?

This is just one of the many reasons the former Secretary of State Hillary Clinton stepped down from her position. She doesn't want to place her political career in jeopardy as she prepares to make a run for the presidency. All of these looming issues are bound to drag her future career into the political abyss. Every Democrat in the Senate and the House of Representatives is fully aware that these issues are going to destroy their chances in the next election. The only thing they can do at this point is stay clear of the Democratic elite in the Senate and blame their Republican Party counterparts in the House of Representatives in order to keep their own political careers from taking a nose dive.

It will be necessary for the OIG to make sure that the HHS hire in CISAs or Certified Information Systems Auditors to make sure the computer systems and the software is protected before the ACA can even be implemented properly. If both parties fail to come to an agreement concerning how to completely rewrite the ACA then the citizens of the United States of America would be the ones who it will hurt the most. If the Republican Party wins we all still would have lost as the country's rating would have been diminished further and we would still not be any closer to fixing the debt ceiling or properly protecting social security numbers and the personal data of our citizens.

4 CHECKS AND BALANCES

Many members of the Republican Party leadership feel that the Clean CR or Clean Continuing Resolution cannot be given to the President of the United States because the United States Government is all about checks and balances. There are several pieces of the Obamacare law inside of the Clean Continuing Resolution which will further damage the U.S. economy.

Republican Congressman Dan Benishek of Michigan stated on the floor of the House of Representatives during the government shutdown in October that getting the Clean CR or Clean Continuing Resolution means that the President of the United States doesn't have to get any approval before changing laws. Checks and balances are necessary "With the Clear CR, It allows the President of the United States to change the law anytime he wants." This can have very serious consequences if not kept in check by the House of Representatives.

Amazingly the Senate Democrats have called the Republicans in the House, "Tea Party Radicals." During the government shutdown in October Republican Congressman Ted Yoho of Florida mentioned that "it has been 237 years since we were told by a dictatorial government that we must buy their tea and pay their taxes."

What is funny about calling the Republicans in the House Tea Party Radicals is that the United States of America was founded to stop dictators from doing what President Obama is trying to do with the U-ACA. The Un-affordable Care Act is trying to make everyone in this country buy their Tea / Insurance and make everyone pay their taxes. Some people feel that this will make this country "a police state."

When people start refusing to sign up for Obamacare the IRS will be tasked with fining American citizens who refuse to use it and could be thrown in jail. Most Democrats for the most part believe in big government but not necessarily forcing people to do what they want. This is not what is meant by being democratic.

Obamacare failed to signed up even 6 people through the website on the first day it went public. If a company which does business on the world wide web only sold 6 products on its first day it would be considered a failure and would have went out of business by now.

This country is strongest when it is allowed to let its' citizens volunteer for the benefits and the needs it is being offered. The Senate and the House need to rewrite the ACA to make it open for everyone who wants it and to take Obamacare as voluntary only and not force people to take it. Our military is an all-volunteer force and we are still considered one of the greatest military powers in the world.

The bigger our government gets, the more power it will be able to wield causing more stress to its' citizens. How many more liberties will be taken away as the government increases its' power over the people? This is a nation with a government, not a government with a nation to govern. We do not want our government telling us what to do and when to do it.

It is in our best interests to select whether we want to select our own insurance company or select what the U.S. government offers for affordable or Un-affordable health care. If President Obama really wants to retain his legacy then he should not further damage the Democratic Party leadership or his Administration. President Obama will need to relinquish his control over the ACA entirely so it can become what Congressman Joe Barton of Texas calls for the wording of the "all voluntary insurance instead of mandatory insurance."

This makes perfect sense and would easily open up the people to select the kind of coverage they want to use. President Obama really pushed to get Obamacare law passed quickly so he could follow through with his campaign promises to help the people who were not being helped. It is admirable for President Obama to help those who have never been helped to have some insurance. What is dangerous is when you prepare legislation and the document leading to that legislation is 2,572 pages long and no one has read it prior to voting as to whether this will assist each and every person in this country as President Obama promised in his campaigns.

Congressman Ralph Hall from Texas stated that "Obamacare regulates all your medical needs and forces people to buy insurance they can't use and premiums they can't afford." This would give the IRS control of your health and your medical care. What genius came up with this policy? Passing a law that makes people use your insurance and taxing them if they don't seems a lot like someone is trying to pay back some constituents for putting them into office. Strange that the people who wrote the website for the ACA just happen to be one of the largest contributors to President Obama's campaign run for the Whitehouse. Looks like he is paying back his supporters by hurting the people who voted him into office at the same time.

This also seems true of these additional 1100 Special Interest Groups that President Obama wants to fund this year. More of the people who gave to his campaign for president? It sounds more like what I would call "Lemonade Stand Politics rather than responsible and honorable representation for our people. It is really odd that no one is hearing anything about these 1100 interest groups now that the Clean CR has been given. With our looming 17 trillion dollar debt President Obama seems undaunted by the massive debt we have accumulated and is still pushing to support all these special interest groups that have nothing to do with protecting U.S. citizens and the president is continuing to spend more money to fund these interest groups in spite of our over-extended debts seemingly out of control.

During the government shutdown Congressman Steve Stockman from Texas stated, "Why is the President of the United States negotiating with the President of Iran, the President of Syria and the Leader of the Terrorists, under the Taliban? They have all outwardly spoken of wanting to kill Americans but President Obama would rather speak to them and refuse to speak with Republican leadership in his own Country."

If the President of the United States thinks this new health care plan is written so perfect why is he refusing to join it instead of using his own health plan? Is it because he doesn't want to use an affordable health care that doesn't take care of his health and raises his premiums to a level he can ill afford? Why is he trying to make the United States follow a law that has no ability to take care of its' citizens? Is it because he is trying to give the funding to those who put him back in office and he needs to pay them back?

Another leader spoke during the government shutdown and I can only imagine how many hundreds of thousands of Americans could be heard in the coffee shops and local restaurants across this nation. Congressman Louie Gohmert from Texas stated on the House floor, "This government is wanting to fund 1100 Special Interest Groups this year. This Commander in Chief has told his military leaders to stop the Catholic Priests from having Mass on Sundays. A person who treats our military veterans badly we do not want running our country or health care."

"Since the Government shutdown the Park Service and they have been told to close down all Veteran Memorials and Veteran Cemeteries so our veterans cannot visit their fallen comrades. This is not who you want running your health care or your country." Disrespecting those who have fought and died to keep this country free from tyranny is an Abomination. This is a serious insult from the Political leader of the free world. Using dead soldiers, cemeteries and memorials as pawns to push your own agenda is sacrilege.

This has nothing to do with which party you support. This has to do with protecting people's rights to choose whether they want health care with one provider or no providers. Not making them take one even if they don't want it. Is the right of every American in this country. This promise which the President of the United States made sure he passed into law has become his promise to assist those without medical coverage even if they do not want it.

Everyone that works an hourly position including Independents and Democrats in this country are now feeling the economic crunch because their jobs have been eliminated or their hours cut. They too no longer feel that Obamacare is such a good idea since it has cut 30% of their pay annually.

Now they need to get another job to pay the debts that continue to accumulate. The ACA has not fulfilled the promises President Obama said it would. President Obama promised the American people that anyone who has insurance and a medical doctor would not lose them, this is no longer the case. Obamacare is going to force us to lose our insurance provider, dump our doctor and double our premiums while at the same time we are making 30% less pay a year. This is going to make living in America a very hard prospect.

I do not believe in all honesty that President Obama knew everything that was written into the U-ACA. If you saw the actual size of the Affordable Care Act document which stands at 2,572 pages or approximately 55 inches thick you would know that the President of the United States has not had the time to read it. A document 55 inches thick is roughly 4.5 feet thick. Now that is a large document!

If he knew that Americans were not going to save $2500 dollars minimum per family annually and that they were going to lose their health care provider and their doctor then that would mean that President Obama lied to the American people. I do not believe that President Obama has lied deliberately to the American people. He is trying to help those who cannot help themselves but at what cost?

The rest of us do not need the ACA and it should only be voluntary for everyone in this country. If the wording is not changed by the Senate, House or this presidency then that means they knew full well what they were doing and need to be removed from office before they completely destroy this country.

We do not need new programs or to fund 1100 Special Interest Groups which he is proposing and the American people cannot afford. Knowing that we have more debt now then in all the 236 years of this nation combined is a very bad presidential legacy. Standing behind a law you have fought for and now realize is harming those it was written to help doesn't make any sense. I believe President Obama wants to change it but once backed into a corner he had to defend the law as it stood.

We need to be willing to talk and work together for more bi-partisan support to change the law to continue to help those it was written for without harming the rest of the country. We need to stop worrying about what side we voted for and realize that together the American people do have a voice through a grass roots coalition. We need to continue to know what our Senators and Congress are voting on in our stead. We can no longer let them do business as usual if our country is being driven off the fiscal cliff.

I believe a man as smart as President Obama wants to have a legacy that will reflect his vision for assisting the United States of America. One of his visions is to show the world that the USA is indeed one of the greatest nations in the history of the world. It is unfortunate that the world will usually identify and point out the shortcomings of leaders after they have left office. Forget about who is at fault and let's start to raise a political yell to make our voices heard in the Congress and the Senate!

He has plenty of time in which to resolve the problems that continue to plague the United States of America. If he makes even minor changes to the ACA, Debt Ceiling, Sequestration and the Presidential policies that are presently in place he will succeed at becoming one of the most influential presidents in the 21st Century.

If the Democratic Party elite and President Obama do not heed the mistakes of the past and continue to believe the political rhetoric his advisors are spouting we are going to dump our country in the economic abyss. I personally believe that our allies and international monetary allies and supporters recognize that the Moderate Democrats and Republicans really want to fix our economic problems and will want our country to pay our debts and change the political landscape in the next election.

You can bet the entire world is paying attention to the economic problems of the USA. If we vote another Democrat into the Whitehouse they had better be a moderate that can work from both sides of the aisle. They had better be a person that can understand that the people of this country are already suffering and do not need their civil rights taken from them.

If we do not step up to the plate and stand for the protection of our citizens and their rights then this country will continue to falter and there will be no way to solve the issues that plague our once great nation. We have a larger government now then we have had over the last 20 years and it is not protecting our civil liberties.

We need to stop setting up programs that are costing our country more money we cannot afford to spend. One of the best reasons our government needs to operate with a balanced budget is in order to stay within that budget. The Senate has called for a budget more than a few times and one of the only people able to create such a document is Republican Paul Ryan from Wisconsin. He should clearly be one of the next front runners for the presidency due to his understanding of the economic infrastructure of this country.

5 HOW TO FIX THE ACA

Firstly, in order to fix what is wrong with the Affordable Care Act or ACA one needs to know what is wrong with the ACA. How does one go about finding what is wrong with the ACA? We can use a set of generic questions which will encompass what has been wrong with health care coverage in North America in order to arrive at a series of numbers in which to analyze how those numbers relate to the new ACA.

We can also get a panel of doctors, hospital administrators and the Health and Human Services to provide the research they have already collected and identify what this new law was supposed to provide which had not been taken care of by previous health care coverage for those who are under insured.

Most of this has been done by the President's advisors and other law makers in the Senate to be given the go ahead to use the data at their disposal to write a new law.   This new law would provide an all-encompassing health care plan that would take care of the medical needs of the American people. The only problem is while they were setting up this new law they added some other initiatives that have nothing at all to do with health. It might appear at first to be helpful to those who are under insured unfortunately it actually backfired and caused a whole new set of problems that could not have been anticipated..

Secondly the reason they cannot easily be fixed has to do with the way the law works and what must be done by a vote in the Senate and the House to change laws that do not work and are not assisting those it was written to protect. We know that President Obama has not read this new law but his advisors only gave him the highlights they considered important.

We know that several lawmakers worked together to create the affordable Care Act into law. The reason we know it had to be done by at least 5+ people is due to its size. No president in office has the time to sit down and read 2,572 pages of a law. The president uses his advisors to give him an understanding of the bill without putting him into harm' s way and also provides deniability. If the law doesn't work out the way President Obama wanted it to, it is plausible that he might not have known all the facts and could deny not having the information necessary to make correct decisions concerning it.

This doesn't hold up to scrutiny. He is the President of the United States of America and the buck must stop with him. Whether he has all the facts or not he is still ultimately responsible for the issues, problems and circumstances he finds himself in during his presidency. He may not think that his children will have to worry about having to use Obamacare but if it is setup and everyone in this country has to use it his grandchildren may be stuck using it as well. If he doesn't fix these laws he has set in motion they will cost him historical controversy, make other presidential failures small in comparison but it may also cost President Obama the loss of his legacy. The ACA has underlying issues in the law that provides a way to circumvent the law and save money on their bottom line.

Due to the ACA, all businesses that use to give their hourly workers 40 hours a week and no benefits are now having to provide benefits. The businesses realized that by cutting their employees hours they still do not have to pay for benefits or insurance. The Obama Administration realized during the government shutdown that they needed to extend the employer mandate to avoid having to worry about it during his own presidency.

If he leaves Obamacare the way it is he will undoubtedly cost the Democrats the Whitehouse in the next election. One thing history has already proven in the United States of America is that the people will rise up if they feel that their rights are in jeopardy. There are approximately 21 States in the America right now presently deciding if they are going to separate from the Union. This is happening because the ACA is placing more power into the hands of the government to control the people.

The president's staff are notorious for under-estimating the statistics and amounts of people who are harmed by circumstances and issues they create. President Obama's Press Secretary identified that only 5% of the population of the United States would be affected by the issues that are incorrect in the ACA and Obamacare. They under-estimated by at least 5 percentage points which means on average that at least 10% of the American population have had their hours cut annually by at least 30% and this is going to cause enormous problems.

What this means is that a minimum of 32,500,000 people or at least 10% of this country have lost their hours which have now been cut from 40 to 28 hours a week or 30% of their annual income. If every company in the United States has now cut the hours of their hourly workers this will be one of the worst U.S. economic disasters this country has ever seen.

That is a loss of 30% of their annual pay and the federal government and the IRS will also receive less money in taxes. This also means that in future administrations they will have to raise more taxes and the working class and small businesses will end up footing that bill as well. This will also mean bigger government which is exactly what Democrats are going to want to do even if we do not need it.

Being independent I recognize that unless the Republicans and the Democrats work together to fix the ACA the Internal Revenue Service and the government will need to raise our taxes to pay for all these programs we can't afford. If the Republican Party continues their rhetoric and continues to try to force the ACA to be repealed and shutdown the Democrats will hold their ground and refuse to change a single word of it even if it is wrong and needs at least to be changed rather than repealed. Why doesn't both sides stop worrying about brinkmanship and instead work to change those sections of the wording that will provide the changes necessary to fix the ACA and at least make it voluntary.

Obamacare is being used by the Democrats to identify that the next president should also be a Democrat. The problem is another Democrat spouting the same needs for big government are only going to cause more problems heading down the wrong direction. The president wants his health plan to work. There are so many other problems involved with it and it is not just Obamacare that has failed but the problems with the debt ceiling, needing to pay our debts and sequestration that is putting our soldiers around the world at risk for no reason. We need to take the critical needs of our infrastructure and military logistical programs off the table as we continue to use sequestration.

Sequestration was written to keep America from spending too much money for instance during a war. It will not work and might even cost human lives around the world when the sequestration stops the military with providing fuel for their troops, their armored personnel carriers, their tanks, their helicopters, etc. When convoys bringing in supplies, food and water to military bases are stopped due to sequestration how many troops need to lose their lives before sequestration will take the military and critical needs off the sequestration table and make sure their funds will not be turned off.

President Obama only needs to tell his advisors and Democratic Senatorial lawmakers that he wants the wording to be changed within the ACA and they will do it. If President Obama wants his legacy to remain in-tact he will need to have the wording of the ACA to reflect sequestration needs to not be connected to critical utilities, military or to any supplies on any post or base. This would certainly go a long way in keeping America protected and that would be one less problem within the ACA.

We really also need to raise the bar on how many hours an hourly must work before they are given insurance and benefits such as instead of 30 hours a week it should be more like 60 hours a week before they are given benefits and insurance. All hourly employees must have their hours given back to them despite who was at fault in the House or the Senate. They need their 40 hours a week returned to them even if they still do not have insurance or benefits. It is imperative that the law be changed to reflect that anyone who works not 30 hours but 60 hours will automatically be given insurance and benefits.

This is not brain surgery and it doesn't take an economist to see that this one change will get America back on its' feet sooner rather than later. It will also mean a devastating blow on the taxes which would have been paid to all the government programs and services across the USA.

Those who already get insurance and benefits for working 40 hours or more are left in place and will continue to keep their insurance if they want to keep it. Those who have not been given any insurance or benefits should not have their hours cut down from 40 hours a week because it will absolutely destroy their future and the future of their children. This has the potential of destroying the economic fabric of the USA.

Anyone who does not want to sign up for the ACA should not have their doctors or their insurance dumped. This must be given back to the people of the USA and without any fines incurred. This is not because it should be done, this is because it has to be done by both the Senate and the House of Representatives.

If any politicians think Obamacare is fine and will not increase the Debt or the Debt Ceiling. Wait six months to a year from now when 50% of the American people will lose their ability to pay their debt, credit cards, mortgages, car payments, gasoline, car insurance and finally will not be able to afford vacations or even food on the table.

It is presently only 32,500,000 people who have had their pay cut by 30% annually because they no longer work 40 hours a week. Their hours are now cut to 28 hours a week which means they have lost 600 hours out of the standard 2000 annual or approximately 30% of their annual pay. I cannot stress enough how much this revenue was needed by working class families and single parent homes.

What will this mean in taxes that will no longer be paid to the Local, County, State or Federal Government? It will mean that the government will be collecting a great deal less taxes from all the citizens and you can bet this will affect the bottom line of this country to pay their debt and to grow the future economy of the U.S. who relied upon it. We are missing something else. The employer mandate will give large and small businesses the opportunity to cut the hours of all employees and at the same time will eliminate the need to pay all benefits and insurance. Why would employers do this? It will keep their money in their pockets and will open up avenues for them to make more money over time.

Let's not continue on this dangerous path of economic destruction.

Obamacare is quite literally going to set this country back almost 100 years by forcing us all to lose our doctors and our providers? What will be next? The U-ACA or Un-affordable Care Act as it is now being called is telling people that not only are you going to lose your health care provider but your doctor as well. You will also be paying twice as much for your insurance and you will only be allowed to pick a doctor from inside the ACA exchanges.

This is ridiculous and personally every man, woman and child in the United States would be screaming in the street if they were not so scared about losing the hours and their jobs due to this train wreck of a law. Obamacare has epic disaster written all over it. The numbers are far more serious than the Press Secretary and the Democrats want the American people to know about.

If 10% of the people in this country lose their jobs over the wording of the Obamacare and then another 10% have their pay cut then we are talking about a minimum of 65,000,000 people who have had their jobs and or their hours cut. How many people in the USA need to lose their jobs or have their hours severely cut before the Senate and the House will wake up and realize that if they can reword it they need to do it shortly before the next election so they can redeem themselves before they are all booted out of office

One question to all politicians in this country including the Senate, the Congress, the President of the United States of America and his cabinet. How many people have to lose their jobs, their pay, their hours, their doctors, their providers and their dignity before any of you will realize the ACA needs to change? We need to change the ACA to reflect that a person must work up to 60 hours a week before they are given benefits and insurance. It is not the right answer when companies all across the nation cut back the hours of hardworking men and women and take 30% of their pay per year and now they are being told they will have to find a way to make their ends meet even though they were already barely getting by before Obamacare ACA law was passed in the Senate.

President Obama has setup the ACA to assist all those who have never had insurance or a doctor before. We know that this new law has created all of these exchanges and the law to help the American people. There is no doubt that people in the USA are apprehensive concerning this new law and that one day it may work out the way it was intended to be but we may have to wait a while before it properly starts to work.

If it is not helping the people you promised to help are you really going to leave it in place even though the people will be oppressed by these changes in their insurance? These are the people who voted for you. They are from the Republican and the Democratic party.

Congressman Mike Conaway from Texas during the government

shutdown stated that "we need to be telling Senator Harry Reid the same words spoken by President Ronald Reagan to President Gorbachev of Russia, "Tear down this wall," of how the Obamacare is written and write it again in such a way that anyone who needs insurance and a doctor can use the ACA Exchanges voluntarily to find a doctor.

I have not heard any Senate or House Democrats speaking against their own party or stating anything at all about how atrocious and dangerous this law will be in the coming years. Not only is it damaging the middle-class but the poor as well and could threaten to destroy small businesses in America. Small business in America is what built this country.

These are the same people that crossed party lines to vote for President Obama because they believed he would protect them and give them a better future. If he does nothing and refuses to have his inner cabinet or invisible counsel change the wording of the ACA or Democratic Senator Reid change the wording of the ACA law to reflect that citizens should not have any hours cut.

Then the law was not written correctly and should be repealed. If the law can be changed to reflect that the hours be given back to hard working Americans up to the 40 hour pay limits then this could create a win-win scenario. If the Democrats in the Senate and the House are not speaking at all does this mean they agree with U-ACA and Obamacare? Why should anyone vote for any Democratic leaders when they have this single point in time to speak out and they have said nothing? The 5th day of the shutdown the President and later the Democratic Party in the House and the Senate started calling this the Republican Shutdown even though it was perpetrated by President Obama and the Democratic elite in the Senate. It is President Obama's goal to force this new law into place.

President Obama used his silence as coercive diplomacy for the 17 days the government was shutdown. Coercive diplomacy is used in international negotiations to force the hand of other governments when you are demanding change against their efforts and to control others.

Democrats saw this as a way to damage the Republican Party and create an avenue to help Hillary Clinton have a better run for the presidency knowing full well that the Republican Party had passed more than 100+ bills in the House of Representatives in order to open up the government without letting go of the Clean Continuing Resolution.

I find it very hard to believe that the Democratic Party and the President has been so transfixed on forcing the ACA on every citizen. We know it is not affordable nor reliable and the President and the Senate have both opted out so they don't have to take this insurance. They seem bound and determined to make the rest of us use insurance we don't need and can't afford. If we refuse to use it they will tax us as though this country was in a police state or run by another dictator.

Why can't the Republican officials in the Senate and the House go back to the Supreme Court and demand that we re-look at the rights of the American people and whether their civil liberties have been violated and that the ACA law is unconstitutional? Why should the American people be forced to sign-up for a law that no longer gives them the right to choose?

How many rights and laws have been circumvented or allowed to be broken before the Supreme Court will rule in favor of the people that the Constitution was written to protect.? I declare that it is also the Declaration of Independence that was also written to protect the people not the government. It is we the people, not we the government and as long as we have the Declaration of Independence and the Constitution of the United States of America it is unlawful for the Supreme Court to rule in favor of a law that circumvents the civil liberties of the people of the United States of America.

Why are we letting this go and not telling our leaders to stop this ridiculous law from going forward? Why has the President of the United States of America damaged relations with our own allies? How many people in this country need to have their lives destroyed, their insurance dumped, their doctors taken, their premiums doubled or tripled, their pay cut and their jobs lost before our officials in the Senate and the House stop this law from proceeding further?

This sounds very much like what King George tried to do to the American Colonists and brought about the Boston Tea Party. We refused at that time to be forced to buy a dictator's tea and pay his taxes. It has only taken 237 years but we have come full circle and are now seeing another dictator telling us we must buy his insurance that we don't need and can't afford and if we don't pay, we must pay his taxes. There are going to be riots in the streets if we do not change this ridiculous wording to incorporate all of these changes as voluntary.

The whole reason for this country is to be free from tyranny. Here we are today and we have another looming tyranny called greed trying to rule this country and is demanding that all insurance carriers drop their customers without any plausible or fair rights for all. Everyone needs to stand up for the rights of all Americans. It is un-American to force anyone in this country to take what they don't need and pay taxes they don't owe just so someone can show the rest of the world that they rule this country.

Maybe we need to seek another Supreme Court ruling so the people will not have their rights trampled so big government can take away more civil liberties. When President Obama decided that he was being put in a corner by Republican Party members who refused to give him the Clean CR he told the Republicans that he was no longer negotiating. The Clean CR does not have to be given, in order for the country to continue to stay open for business.

The President only had to accept a partial opening for 6 weeks by the Temporary Clean CR or Continuing Resolution. He decided to stop the Senate from voting for any of the more than 100+ incremental bills that the House Republicans had already passed 5 days prior to keep the government open. President Obama refused to take a 6 week temporary CR – he forced the United States Government to shut down. Let me say that again...

The reason we had a shutdown was due to a bit of a temper tantrum on the part of the President of the United States demanding that the House give him a Clean CR or else. Saying either you give me what I want or I will not negotiate with you. This was a ploy setup by our Commander in Chief, President Obama by his inner advisors or invisible counsel to create a problem as a way to disparage the Republicans in the House and the Senate and create an unnecessary shutdown to make the Republican Party members lose popularity so they will not be as strong in the next election when Hillary Clinton takes her run at the presidency.

This is only my opinion but what other reason would the President of the United States have to shut down the government when he was already given the Clean CR for 6 weeks? Could it be that since he had the lowest ratings in history of a Democratic President he might be trying to bring up his ratings and using this opportunity to damage the reputations of the Republican Party leadership at the same time? This is quite plausible and would even bring up the ratings of the President if he could create enough of a spin in the media to blame the Republican Party for the problems we are now facing.

Please realize that without the Republican Party leadership in place to make sure that President Obama does not overstep his responsibilities on the Sequestration, the Debt-Ceiling, Clean CR, and keeping the Government open, President Obama has seen his ratings continue to fall by 40%. Why not work together to alleviate these massive issues that now looms over our present government and its' people?

Not even 1 Democrat has spoken out against the Un-affordable Care Act. Not even 1 person out of hundreds of Democrats. They are falling behind their leadership and brinkmanship, following the Democratic Party leadership status quo knowing that they are all going to be seen as nothing more than followers. Is there no leaders among all of the so-called moderates who are willing to talk with Republicans in the House or the Senate?

It is amazing the kind of power that President Obama is wielding in the Whitehouse. Most Democrats have never seen this kind of sandbagging by any previous administrations. He has really made sure that he hand-picked the Democratic Party leadership to spout the all to familiar rhetoric and at the same time have them act as though they are bending over backward to assist the Republican Party who it just so happens did pass more than 100+ incremental bills to keep the government running.

If the moderate Democrats that really wanted to work with their political rivals across the aisle had helped pass the incremental bills sent to the Senate floor by the House of Representatives than President Obama would not have been able to sandbag the Republican Party leadership and the government would have been open for business before the shutdown.

With Democratic Party leadership such as Senator Reid and Representative Pelosi keeping their party towing the line or kowtowing to their leadership it is no wonder that no one spoke out of turn. They are going to have a real fight on their hands to stay in office once the people start to realize that they have been duped. It no longer matters what party you belong to, the people need to have their 40 hours returned to them. We need to have our civil liberties returned to us and be given the right to turn down the ACA if we choose to say <u>No</u>!

Speaking about Obamacare as it is commonly called will bring up other topics that are beginning to affect and influence how President Obama is perceived by his constituents and his party. The President can only blame the Republicans in the House of Representatives for just so long. Logically he is not going to be able to continue to ridicule others and Republican Representative John Boehner for very long without bringing attention to the fact that he was refusing to negotiate.

As we know after the U.S. Government opened back up for business many moderate Democrats started to cite with their rivals in the Republican Party due to the failure of the Obamacare website. They started to realize that the media was starting to point out that Obamacare was not working and the moderate Democrats began to work with their rivals across the aisle to identify to their constituents that they are willing to negotiate.

6 THE FULCRUM OF LEGACY

I believe President Obama will not change his direction or negotiate because these topics are at the fulcrum of his legacy. It is unfortunate that not all intentions workout the way they were initially planned. Sometimes the best laid plans cause problems that were not anticipated by any Parties prior to becoming resolute. The same is true with Obamacare.

The President was unaware that making the ACA or Affordable Care Act into a law was going to destroy incomes and damage the middle-class who put him in office and that most companies in the USA were going to find a work-around by cutting the hours of the American men and women in this country down from 40 hours a week to 28 hours a week. This also means that those people whose hours have been cut are now missing 48 hours a month or approximately one third of their annual income.

What none of us anticipated is that President Obama was going to play hardball over the ACA to such a degree that he was not interested in changing a single word of a law with 2,572 pages in it. Obamacare on its' own will single-handedly irreparably damage both the poor and the middle-class in this country. Most people in this country are hard-working Americans that want to have a job, pay their bills, take vacations and continue to live in the greatest country in the world. They want to provide for their family and take care of their children.

Political and economic influences from inside and outside President Obama's circle of influence are starting to realize that the unintended consequences of the ACA or Affordable Care Act may be creating additional and daunting problems that must be fixed before it can go forward. Additional issues may stem from the way the ACA was originally written.

Unfortunately President Obama, Senator Harry Reid and Representative Nancy Pelosi have made it all too clear that they have no intention of changing any of the wording of the Affordable Care Act and will not negotiate concerning it. Their stance is seen by most people in this country as extreme to say the least.

President Obama made it a point to Call for Conference so Congressman Boehner would go to the Whitehouse and the president could tell him to his face that he was not going to negotiate or even speak with him over the Affordable Care Act until the House Republicans gave a Clean CR or Clean Continuing Resolution which would mean that the President of the United States could continue to run the United States as business as usual or into the ground by wasting more additional monies. The only problem with a Clean CR is that we no longer can afford to just continue as usual.

The United States of America has several looming catastrophic problems that must be dealt with in short order to avoid defaulting on our 17 trillion dollar deficit. Make no mistake about it, these problems are real and they were partially created by other previous presidents before President Obama became our President. His current presidency has continued our spiral of debt and our debt is now quadrupled. Let me say that again, since President Obama came to the Whitehouse our debt is now 4 X larger than when he first entered office.

Most people in this country 20 years ago didn't understand what 1 billion pieces of computer data or a gigabyte of data was and now the average person knows what a terra-byte is in terms of hard drive space. 1 trillion dollars is equal to 999 Billion + 1 Billion more or $1,000,000,000,000. This number is astronomical and that we owe 17 trillion is unheard of anywhere. It is obvious that our continuing debt was created by several past presidents and by getting involved with other countries political and military affairs as well as supporting our allies.

Our debt has now reached epic proportions. All of these issues are now part of this presidency and we need to make sound decisions to avoid crippling our own present circumstances and our children's future. It is unfortunate that President Obama did not feel obligated to Call for Conference to discuss the ACA with Republicans in the House just before the shutdown. He also knew that House Republicans could stall the legislation indefinitely and therefore decided to push it through without their input. What is interesting is that House Republicans would have been interested in looking at ACA and possibly rewriting sections to make it better.

President Obama had already heard the rhetoric from his right wing colleagues and knew the Republicans were not going to let the ACA legislation pass. His invisible counsel of inner circle advisors would have made it very clear that if he wanted to get this law to pass they would have to try a more unconventional approach. He had probably decided before ever trying to send the law to the floor of the House that it would not pass and made the decision to do it without the Republican support or any

Republican votes in the Senate.

The moderates in the Republican Party were not given any heads up from moderate Democrats that the Democrats were going to bring any bill to the floor of the Senate on Christmas Eve. There is no way to definitively identify what the Democratic leadership told their members in the Senate to get them to tow the line, stay silent and stay in Washington D.C. on Christmas Eve. The President's invisible counsel of inner circle advisors must have known who needed to know early before they kept everyone at the beginning of the Christmas break. Senator Reid and Democratic leadership had to have known more than a month in advance what they were going to do and formulated how to handle the moderate Democrats as well as quell any complaints or problem Democrats long before the Christmas Holiday. It was interesting how little media attention was paid to this manner of political maneuvering to circumvent the Republicans in the Senate or the House from even knowing about their agenda for Christmas Eve.

There is no telling whether Republicans in the House or the Senate would have taken a longer look at the ACA if there was more justifiable reasons for having an Affordable Care Act. If millions of people were to call in, write in, or create a grass roots effort to bring attention to this need it is possible that Republican moderates would have been interested in discussing it. I am certain they would have found merit in the legislation and would have assisted to help the people it was originally intended for if there were any people it could assist. He was determined to make sure that the ACA was passed on Christmas Eve to avoid any Republicans trying to stop the ACA from becoming a law. He was able to pass the legislation without a single vote from the Republican Party.

When the President of the United States and the Democrats in the Senate requested the Clean Continuing Resolution in September of 2013 which is necessary to keep the government open and continue to move forward Congressman Boehner and House Republican Leadership recognized a way to stop the President of the United States from pushing any more of the ACA on the people of the United States.

They decided to start Sandbagging President Obama in order to stop him from maneuvering further into debt and get him to discuss the need to take a more realistic and responsible approach to our looming debt ceiling. The Republicans wanted to have the ACA debate and the rewrites and talks with bi-partisan law makers before they signed it into law. Now that it has already passed into law we need to take another look at what they are now calling either Obamacare or the Un-affordable Care Act.

The Republican and Democrat constituents are smart enough to realize that it was not the Republican Party alone that created the shutdown of the Government. Many American people only see Obamacare as another foolish idea that is going to cost the middle-class more of their pay towards taxes. Why is it not obvious to the politicians in America that big and small business are going to do whatever is necessary to save money and keep more of it in their pockets. This new law has now opened another gap for businesses and at the same time caused the average American family to be burned again by limiting their ability to pay their bills. The average household was working forty hours a week and getting limited or no insurance.

By placing more restrictions on large and small businesses it only created another solution for large businesses to avoid paying their workers full time. Getting businesses to shutdown altogether to avoid any other restrictions or getting fined for not taking care of all their workers including their hourly employees is now causing huge issues across the USA.   Now that the average American household is no longer working 40 hours a week but instead 28 hours a week they will not be able to continue to pay their bills, pay their taxes, pay their mortgages, pay for vacations, or pay utilities.

I wonder if President Obama would have a problem if his pay of $400,000 was cut by 30% annually and he was now making $280,000 dollars? He was then told he needs to drop his doctor and select a new health care plan and doctor. How would President Obama feel if he was told he would be fined if he did not use the new Navigator Exchange to pick a new medical coverage and get a new doctor? As an added bonus President Obama would have to choose whether to pay for his medicine or his meals but not both.

Please do not tell me that every American in this country can keep their doctor and whatever insurance package they already use and then act as though you care about the American people when you have gone out of your way to make sure that you have at least three full layers of advisors to protect your deniability when it all doesn't work out in your Party's favor.

The American people have rights too! The Democratic Party should be checking if there is a way to fix these huge problems with either bi-partisan assistance or revamping the U-ACA before the Republican Party takes the initiative to repeal the U-ACA or Obamacare. The in-dependents out there need to put their efforts towards building a grassroots effort to make sure all members of the Senate, and the House cannot avoid the issues.

If we can make a "Political Yell," and send a message to all our representatives in Washington, D.C. and locally that we need the ACA completely rewritten to reflect that the people of the United States of America do have a voice. We can use it to change the direction of this very bad and damaging law from destroying our lives, costing us our homes, our livelihoods, our sanity, our pay, our futures, our children's future.

How many people's lives have to be damaged or destroyed before the government of the people and by the people step up and do the honorable thing and protect the American people and our way of life. If the law is so perfect why did President Obama feel it was necessary to change the law more than 10 separate times during last Summer 2013. If the law doesn't need changing why is it that Democrats in the Senate are being notified by their constituents that they want to repeal Obamacare.

7 NEGOTIATION OR DENIAL ?

Does President Obama really think that the people of the United States of America are scared of change and that is why we want to repeal and shutdown Obamacare? A few days before the government completely reopened CNN had an interview with a famous celebrity who shared that "the reason the American people do not want the Affordable Care Act is because they are scared of change."

Really? Is that what a celebrity billionaire really thinks? Well thank God we have celebrity economist billionaires that we can rely on to see through all the rhetoric. I respect your work but I am afraid that you missed the boat on what is happening with Obamacare. Are you kidding? That is what we're scared of...? As an example of what is happening to approximately 65,000,000 people in the United States of America why don't we create a small example by using a portion of a celebrity billionaires in-exhaustive wealth and see if this can shed some light on what these people are facing now that Obamacare is being implemented.

I am just guessing here but let's say that we eliminate this celebrity billionaire's bank accounts so they are also living paycheck to paycheck. If on this celebrity's next feature film where they are both an actor and director instead of making millions of dollars they will only be paid $1000 per week. For the sake of the argument the government is going to take 30% of their monthly pay or $1200 dollars per month and refuse to pay them what they are owed. That worker would throw a temper tantrum.

This is not entirely relative since the celebrity has several billion dollars but if they were told that instead of being allowed to work as many hours as they would like or a 15 hour day, 6 days a week equaling 90 hours they had to quit each week after hitting 28 hours and the rest of their pay was being cut. They wouldn't just be upset, they would have a fit, they would be screaming in the streets.

Now this is only my sentiments but most people are not going to take it lying down without saying something to their representatives in

Washington D.C. At the next election they are going to use their Democratic rights to voice their opinion by voting someone else into office who will stop this brinkmanship and put things back to the way they used to be and give back all the hours they were working prior to take care of their family, pets, household and life.

There is no way the people are going to remain silent while their livelihoods and there futures are being tossed upon the rocks of change. We are not scared of change, we are scared of not being able to take care of our children, our parents, our households, our mortgages, our utilities, our food, our clothes. In short, we are angry that the government is no longer acting for the best interests of the American people. We are <u>not</u> scared of change, we are asking for changes be made to the Affordable Care Act to make it entirely voluntary. That every hourly person who works 60 hours a week or more be entitled to benefits and insurance. That no one should have their hours cut back to 28 hours a week when they want to work 40 hours or more a week. We know that the average person who works full time normally works 40 hours a week. We also know that the average person who is a full time employee is salaried and oftentimes works longer than the usual 40 hours during the week.

You might say this is not happening but I tell you that is exactly what is happening. The businesses in this country are either taking the hours from their hourly staff or they are eliminating the jobs entirely which means at least 65,000,000 people's lives are being put in peril over legislation. Please realize Miss Celebrity that I do not mean any disrespect to you. I just think that you may not have all the facts and without them your conclusion is flawed and your logic is unsound.

The people in this country are going to voice their opinions during the next election which will mean that the Democratic moderates who said nothing when their political elite told them to tow-the-line are going to face the fight of their political lives as the people in the United States are going to want to put in a Republican President, Senate and House in order to make sure that this is repealed, de-funded and shutdown before it destroys this country. As an independent I recognize that if we get enough votes from the conservative side we will split the vote but the same is true on the liberal side. I would rather think that independents are smart enough to run for office from within one of the existing political parties and work within Washington, D.C. as a moderate no matter what side of the aisle they find themselves.

President Obama's Invisible Counsel of advisors were running out of ideas to push the Republican leadership into giving in to the President's demands instead of negotiating before the government shutdown.   It really seems that the President's advisors were not just giving their advice to the President but also to Democratic leadership who came out to the microphones after the Call for Conference to share with the media that they were giving all the concessions the Republican Party wanted and still the Republican Party leadership were not willing to talk.

The average American can see right through these ploys and only wants the Senate, the House and the President to do what is necessary to protect our way of life. It is obvious to the American people that the President of the United States was not negotiating but in complete denial.

It seems strange to think that the President of the United States of America would communicate with the President of Iran on the same day as the Call For Conference knowing this is a slap in the face to the President's own Democratic leadership but it does appear that President Obama's advisors or Invisible Counsel clearly wanted to show that the President could continue with his duties no matter what was happening within the House or the Senate.

The President failed to communicate with our allies or even with Israel, Great Britain, Germany or France. Why would the leader of the free world not talk with our own allies? Iran's previous leaders have promised to kill Americans. They have denied the Holocaust perpetrated by the Nazis against the Israeli people. Even within the Koran it states that a Muslim is allowed to lie about facts in order to protect their religious rights.

This is why it is dangerous for the President of the United States and the Secretary of State to make deals with Iran. The agreement you are making says they can no longer make nuclear material but their interpretation states that this deal gives them the freedom to make nuclear material and continue to pursue the building of a nuclear weapons arsenal in order to use it to kill the Israeli people and their allies.

The Israeli people are our allies and dear friends of the United States of America. We need to remain in close contact and continue to keep a close and firm commitment to those who live in Israel. The Administration of this presidency and the Senate is walking a dangerous obstacle course not protecting the American people and their futures. Our leaders have to know that this may not affect them but it will affect their children's children' s children.

If we do not back-pedal and fix the wording of the ACA or Obamacare this country could quite possibly turn on itself. There are literally millions of people in the United States today who no longer have any health insurance because when ACA was enacted it changed their lives overnight. Yes, everyone in America knows that each time there is a mandate it costs us our civil liberties. How many civil liberties will be trampled by this new ACA law?

Big business and not-for-profits are cutting hourly workers hours below 29 hours so they can avoid paying fines for not providing insurance and benefits they have no intention of paying. To make it easier to remain below they set the hours at 28 per week. Anyone who cares about these hourly workers understand that their children or their children's children have to know that these hours are going to make their future worse as well.

Anyone who was an hourly full time worker has had their hours cut and can no longer afford to pay their medical bills, medical prescriptions or put food on the table. Now they will have to make a decision on what will be the most important thing to buy or they will need to now work 2 or maybe even 3 jobs to fill the hours lost. Any hourly workers in this country will no longer be able to afford to take vacations and the tourism businesses are going to suffer terrible losses due to the lack of tourists in our own country.

This will create a lack of vacations from the middle-class who can no longer afford one, lack of new small businesses, lack of money, lack of future earnings, lack of medical coverage and to top it all off no one will be able to afford these losses or insurance premiums. What is going to happen to my children's future if we cannot afford these losses on any level? One of the areas that each elected official should be paying attention to is what is going to happen to my child under this Administration? How many decades do we need to live under these unfair practices while businesses and elected officials remain unaffected?

8 WHO IS SANDBAGGING WHOM ?

President Obama's behavior was perceived by the Republican Party as an insult in the beginning of October. He was not even going to speak with Congressman Boehner unless the House Republicans were willing to let the government open without any concessions and a Clean CR. The House has asked for several concessions and has passed 100+ incremental bills in which to open parts of the US Government which is a reasonable gesture on the part of the House of Representatives.

It is important to point out that several bills have been passed in the House of Representatives and they have been sent to the Senate floor at the beginning of October but Democratic leadership stalled the House in order to get them to give the Clean CR first. This has nothing to do with Senate leadership but that President Obama was trying to control the House Republicans and force them to give the Clean CR so the President could make whatever changes he deems necessary including raising the debt ceiling and continue his spending spree completely free of the checks and balances of the House.

This country can ill afford a U.S. Government that has an Administration that is on a continuous spending spree and is determined to destroy the very fabric of this great nation from within to fund his grand plans. No matter how important initially this original plan might have been, the people all across the USA are starting to feel the crunch and may start to think again that we need to get back to 2004 spending limits. Where we were paying our debts and making strides to bring the debt ceiling under control.

Both television media and on-line media have been scoped on these issues since the first days of the government shutdown on October 1st, 2013. There is a clear reason as to why both the House leadership and the Senate leadership continue to refuse to go forward even though moderates in the House and the Senate want to discuss and work together to re-open the government. The Democratic Party reasoning has to do with following political party lines. Not wanting to bring any attention to their party they remain quiet while the rest of the country is feeling the crunch as millions of people are having their jobs eliminated or many hours cut right out of their pay. Big business sees this as another way to avoid having to pay for insurance and benefits. Did President Obama's speech writer create Obamacare out of thin air? This is the worst piece of legislation to ever come out of any US Political Party. I do not believe this is what former President Bill Clinton and former Secretary of State Hillary Clinton meant by wanting to create a national health care initiative.

Certainly someone of President Obama's character and intelligence knew what he was doing when he let the legislation pass into law. Not everyone becomes a professor of law at the University of Chicago but even with his vast knowledge he let this weak legislation get passed into law. At least one of his advisors must have read the document and explained that several pieces were going to need vast changes and revisions.

What reason could there be to not allow the Republican leadership to negotiate any changes of Obamacare? There are no reasons why the President of the United States shouldn't have tried to have a conference with Republican leaders unless he is fully aware that this legislation is going to destroy the middle-class and small business which were the people who put him in the Oval office in the first place.

It helps no one to vilify the Democrats or the Republican Party leadership in the House of Representatives when sharing controversial problems that we are all facing in the United States. No matter what side we take there is no question that everyone is being hurt by the ACA law economically.

Unless you are independent of the American system or you do not need to work it will directly affect you or your children. In talking to people researching this information I have also spoken to many people about their concern of this issue and everyone no matter what party they are affiliated with do not want ACA to go forward. There are plenty of people who are considered upper-class Chief Executive Officers, Chief Financial Officers of corporations who clearly do not need ACA but it is seriously affecting the bottom-line. Many people are losing their hours but businesses are having to get more people to replace the hours lost and having to get more people trained takes money. Having a need to hire more people continues to add additional responsibilities to make sure companies stay effective and running at optimal levels. Now that people have less work and are not allowed to work over 30 hours puts a strain on those working full time to make up the difference and assure that the work is still completed under budget and on time.

Most people in the United States that work in an hourly position used to work 40 hours a week. Due to the ACA law they will lose 12 hours a week not just 10, the reason for this is that employers want to make sure that their staff do not go over the 30 hours for the week so they have taken more precautions and hours to verify no one goes over the 30 hours identified within the ACA.

This may not seem like a great deal of time but when it is seen in the context of an annual pay it is obvious that these 12 hours per week is monumental. 12 hours per week X on average 50 weeks = 600 hours of pay lost due to the ACA law or .30 percent of annual salaries have just been cut by the Affordable Care Act.

It no longer matters what side or what party you belong to... No one wants to lose 30 % of their salary for any reason when they are already paying nearly 30% in taxes. The ACA law is not going to just devastate your pay but it will stop you from going to see your doctor and you are no longer able to use the insurance you have paid into for years.

This cannot be correct. Why should a U.S. Administration that is no longer protecting their people be allowed to stay in office? It is starting to look as though someone in President Obama's authority read the 2,572 pages of the ACA Law and did not fully explain all the different changes that may occur in relation to this new law.

The President of the United States of America did not write the ACA and whoever is giving him this advice is making a huge mistake. His advisors have got to know that this is a major deal breaker. This is an absolute no-win scenario. It is in the best interests of the Democratic and Republican leadership to come back to the table and discuss how to fix the wording of the ACA in order to give people who do not have medical insurance an opportunity to have it and that those who already have insurance do not lose it by making all of it voluntary only.

The Democratic party stated many times leading up to the government shutdown that they were no longer willing to work with the Republicans from the other side of the aisle or even meet to talk concerning the ACA. This shutdown is one of the most absurd and utterly unnecessary in US history. In listening to Democratic leaders Senator Harry Reid and Representative Nancy Pelosi in front of cameras and using the media as a spin-op, it seems clear they have been coached by President Obama's advisors. In Phillip Geyelin's book (LBJ, p.210) he explains at length that "It was a familiar Johnson stratagem to send known dissenters to argue on behalf of his policies." This could be the same strategic solution that President Obama could have been using to alleviate controversies during the government shutdown.

This is also known by another name used by presidential policy making strategies. In George E. Reedy, The Twilight of the Presidency (New York: World, 1970) and Chester L. Cooper "A formal devil's advocate role would be an artificial and contrived one, empty of real meaning because the advocate is simply role-playing and is not arguing with serious conviction." Throughout the government shutdown at each occurrence that Senator Reid or Representative Pelosi were speaking before the media it seemed painfully obvious that they were not saying anything new but rather were saying that they were willing to talk about anything Congressman Boehner would like to talk about but that he was not willing to talk.

This is a perfect example of a contrived argument or role-playing strategy. In this manner the president would not have to get into a debate over policy decisions but instead he could use dissenters to create political controversy in order to keep his policies in play. If Republicans in the House or the Senate had conflicting policies the president could use multiple dissenters in the House and the Senate to create contrived arguments to keep political rivals at bay while preparing a political counter-strategy.

We have all heard Democrats name calling the Republicans in the House using insults to get one over on the Republican Party leadership. What is obvious to most Americans is that they are simply at fault just as much as the Republicans in office but with one exception. Most Americans want the Republican Party to repeal, shutdown, or defund Obamacare. Republicans need to realize that this may not happen. This is a landmark legacy and President Obama will not be side-stepping or walking away from the table.

Therefore in order to go forward it is absolutely essential for Republicans in the House and the Senate to come together and agree that they need to work to assist the president in fixing the law so his legacy will work and his campaign promises will be fulfilled. It is important at this juncture to lay down your convictions and work with both sides of the aisle to fix the Affordable Care Act law. Everyone on Capitol Hill needs to be willing to work together in bi-partisan committees to make sure the ACA Law will work for the people it was written to protect.

Now that it is being called the Un-affordable Care Act, maybe people need to start calling their Congressman and Senators and tell them that they cannot afford to have their 40 hours cut to 28 hours per week. If the average family is losing 30% of their pay, they are going to lose their house, their cars, their vacations, their medical, their savings and their futures along with approximately 65 million others. The average family is no longer going to spend money on luxuries. They will no longer be interested in wasting time. They are going to take it to the streets and they will see their lives destroyed along with their future and the future of their children's children.

Historically this country has ridden on the back of the working middle class. The middle class and small businesses are what built this country and has made the United States one of the economic powers in the world.

Now through some mistakes by the wording of Obamacare, Americans can no longer afford the insurance they had or the Un-affordable Care they are forced to take. All across the United States of America we are hearing in the media that people now have to pay 2 to 3 times more than previously for the same or worse medical coverage, this is a travesty.

Before Obamacare should ever be implemented it is absolutely imperative to protect American citizens personal data and privacy from being vulnerable on the Health and Human Services computer databases. Testimony was given on March 19th in Washington, D.C. that the HHS had been audited by the Inspector Generals tasked to do audits and the Health and Human Services failed on at least seven separate vulnerabilities which must be fixed before the Affordable Care Act can become implemented or turned on. The only thing created by Health and Human Services to identify solutions was a paper that was written identifying the implementation of what HHS will do to correct the situation. Nothing has been implemented since that time.

The private data of American citizens is highly vulnerable and there are deficiencies, data security is not protected properly, the public health is vulnerable and there are no standards setup to have sufficient Emergency Preparedness in place at any of the 300 locations of HHS in the USA. The following testimony was already given and HHS needs to fix these vulnerabilities before the ACA should be allowed to go further. This would take up to 3 years to complete and would need to be verified by the Inspector General's offices before the ACA would be allowed to activate or fine anyone from giving their personal and private information to the HHS or register for any medical insurance through the exchanges.

Testimony of HHS vulnerabilities :

On the House of Representatives website there is a list of testimony that was given by several people from the Office of Inspector General concerning the U.S. Department of Health and Human Services. It took place March 19th, 2013 at the Rayburn House Office Building in room 2358-C. One of the Inspector Generals was Daniel R. Levinson who gave testimony before the "United States House of Representatives Committee on Appropriations. The Subcommittee on Labor, Health and Human Services, Education and related agencies." The testimony was given concerning many failures on the part of Health and Human Services and the challenges they face.

The Inspector Generals have to inspect the procedures and practices of 300 Health and Human Services or HHS Programs. In his testimony Mr. Levinson identified seven areas that continue to be a problem and are plaguing the Health and Human Services programs. "Deficiencies and vulnerabilities relating to Grants, Contracts, Data Security, Improper Payments as well as the Administration, Emergency Preparedness and Public Health."

These areas are significantly large areas within Health and Human Services and these problems will continue to cause issues which will most certainly affect the Un-affordable Care Act as it is being implemented. How can we move forward in the implementation of ACA, Un-affordable Care Act if none of these issues has yet to be fixed.

According to other testimonies given, the only thing HHS or Health and Human Services did to resolve these problems was to write down a plan to implement. What? How can ACA be allowed to go forward when all these issues have still not been resolved. American citizen's data needs to be sufficiently protected before the ACA law can be safely protected and move forward.

A major vulnerability is not adequately protecting the security of the data of private citizens in the United States of America. Personally I don't think it is right to make anyone accept the Affordable Care Act unless every one of its' citizens have the right to turn it down if they want to do it. It is not only ethically wrong it should be illegal to make anyone buy your tea. What happened to Life, Liberty and the Pursuit of Happiness ?

Not only are we being taken to the cleaners or ripped off by Obamacare or the Un-Affordable Care Act in being forced to lose our insurance carriers but we are being forced to pay as much as 2 or 3 times as much for health care that doesn't provide care or take care of our health. The Democrats say they have spoken to Republican leadership and how they have worked tirelessly to find a common thread that they can work with Republicans in the Senate and the House. It is obvious they are also taking the advice of President Obama's advisors or invisible counsel as they get in front of the media and declare it is all the Republicans fault.

Of course this is nothing but Democratic rhetoric and they are trying to place blame on someone other than themselves. The American people know that the Republican Party had little or nothing to do with the passing of ACA law but they are still wanting the Republicans to fix it all somehow. This will be a monumental undertaking on the part of all political parties to work on the changes that will need to take place to implement this law properly and also make it a voluntary legislation so the American people can live with it and it will be able to assist those it was written to protect.

The Obama Administration tried to force the hand of the Republicans to give up the Clean CR so President Obama could continue to spend and make whatever changes were necessary to go forward as he nears the twilight of his presidency. I hate to tell you the obvious but it takes two to tango. The Republicans did not do this without being backed into a corner by the President of the United States when he decided to refuse any changes even minor changes to the Affordable Care Act. Knowing full well that even minor wording would protect the American people in the United States.

The Democrats and President Obama have also been backed into a corner but through their own measure. So what can we do to stop sandbagging each political party along with the President and get the party leadership back to the table? If I may, let me quote an old adage, we need to get along to go along. We need to give some consideration to what the President is trying to accomplish and open the debt ceiling a little and we need to open negotiations to open government for at least six months so discussions can move forward in the House and the Senate.

9 WHAT'S NEXT ?

This calls into question why Democrats in the Senate or the Republicans in the House are not willing to have these very real issues discussed as we continue to see this looming debt-ceiling? It is time to stop the brinkmanship and start working together in bi-partisan committees to work together to achieve real and lasting affordable care to all U.S. Citizens.

Before we look to lay blame on anyone we need to look at why the Democrats, the Republicans or the President of the United States would appear to be holding back the rest of the country. One thing we might consider is that President Obama was doing everything in his power to help those people in this country that have never had any type of medical insurance or benefits. This is a wonderful ideal.

That is a fine and noble thing he is trying to do but the wording in the ACA should reflect whatever changes are necessary and setup the entire Insurance program to be completely voluntary. The promises President Obama made before the people during his campaign is at the very heart of his legacy and he doesn't want to let the people of the United States miss any opportunities to gain medical coverage or miss out in having benefits and insurance while on their watch. This is a terribly noble position and is a wonderful legacy to retain as he is in the twilight of his presidency. Unfortunately the way Obamacare was written has caused several problems throughout this country. What the wording should say is that anyone who is an hourly worker and works 60 hours or more per week are entitled to insurance and benefits.

Why should it say 60 hours instead of 30? The reason it should say any hourly workers who work 60 hours or more per week has to do with how this has affected working class people in America. Most people in the middle class today work a minimum of 40 hours per week and are given benefits and insurance already. This is reasonable and expected. Most people in the USA who are hourly workers previously were working 40 hours per week as well but were not receiving any benefits or medical insurance. The wording of the ACA limits the hourly workers now to under 30 hours which means they will not only work less hours but also make less pay.

Why do we want to destroy the working class whose votes put President Barack Obama into the Whitehouse? Well the answer is a resounding No. We do not want to destroy the working middle class. That was not the intention of President Obama in my opinion. If President Obama is not in control of his presidency who is pulling his strings at present and can make these changes on the ACA so that the American people can be treated fair and reasonable.

This simply became the problem of the wording of the ACA and in order to keep it from being modified too radically the President and the Democratic party decided to refuse further negotiations in repealing it. The Republican Party needs to change their stance and they need to identify that since the ACA is a law we need to change the wording in order to protect those who already have insurance so they do not have to lose their doctors or their present insurance plans.

The ACA needs to reflect who the law was written to protect. Those who do not work and those who work minimal hours still need medical insurance and benefits. Those who already work 40 hours a week should not have their hours cut or taken from them but simply put, they just need something in place that will give them insurance and benefits when they work 60 or more hours a week. Please realize that it is a safe bet that those who are in leadership positions within the U.S. Government are not the same people who have written these pieces of legislation. The people who draft the initial piece of legislation still need to get the approval of their own party before it can be fully ratified and signed into law.

We know that most laws take several revisions before they can be implemented without problems or flaws. This goes without saying. The President knows this as does the Democratic Party leadership and the Republican Party are also well versed as to why this is necessary.

They spend most of their time in Washington, D.C. creating revisions to laws that are already in place that are not helping those they were originally written to assist. I am convinced that President Obama and the Democratic Party brainstormed, created, wrote and pushed to make health care affordable for all Americans the single most important resolution under his Presidency and his legacy.

He made it his presidential campaign promise and shared with the American people that the average family would save X amount of dollars a year on their health care costs. It is unfortunate that no families have saved any monies due to the Un-Affordable Care Act and only a select number have even tried to seek new insurance at this time. In a very bold move President Obama was virtually catapulted into office with his campaign promises. In all honesty all of us wanted this for our future. We have seen rising costs on almost every level of health care as our health plans continue to diminish.

We need some sort of stop-gap in our rising health care costs so all Americans can afford to take care of their children and provide for their parents as they age. As this law presently stands no one can afford the ACA and if President Obama wants to make it his legacy he may want to rethink his decision making paradigm which may have been flawed if there were no alternatives to its implementation.

People crossed party lines to vote for President Obama and although his rivals Senator John McCain and Governor Mitt Romney among other rivals are good men and had all the skills to achieve fiscal solvency, to strengthen our military, and to work diplomatically most of the people in our country wanted to get back to fixing the problems here at home.

Hillary Clinton had the skills to get the vote. Once it was aware she was not going to be able to win the Democratic Nomination she gave her support to Barack Obama and the rest was history. President Obama made her the Secretary of State. She stepped down more than a year ago to distance herself from the Democratic Party and Obamacare to prepare for her run at the Whitehouse as a candidate.

Once in the Oval Office President Obama started working to create the ACA or Affordable Care Act. He met and spoke with men and women all over this nation as he was campaigning for his bid to be President of the United States. He must have felt compelled to want to work to fix this huge ongoing problem that has seen people all over this nation hurting from the lack of affordable care. The First Lady of the United States of America Mrs. Obama worked in the pharmaceuticals industry and must have seen first-hand that most people in this country cannot afford these very expensive prices for much needed medications.

Now as President Obama has worked through his Presidency. He campaigned and made it one of his promises to the American people. He was going to do everything he could to make Health Care affordable for everyone in the USA. This is a very high ideal and shows the character of President Obama. I believe he is a good man who took it upon himself to make the Un-affordable Care Act a legacy for all Americans. He has followed through with his promises and he should be proud of his legacy. It is also important to realize that things do not always work the way we would like them to whether it be in principal or in practice. Do not judge others if they are different. Let's instead embrace the differences between us so we can honor our diversity.

Economically the ACA, Obamacare or Un-ACA – Un-affordable Care Act is going to cause this Presidency to spend inordinate amounts of money equaling the already funded Medicare and the ACA funds to add another 1.7 trillion to the current deficit. There does not seem to be an end in sight even though the debt ceiling cannot be raised from our current levels.

This administration has created the largest deficit this country has ever seen and more debt than all the previous 237 years combined. The Democrats and the Republicans are using this government shutdown as a bargaining chip in order to get their witch-hunt political rhetoric brought to the attention of the American people.

What is actually going on is that the House Republicans continued to pass nearly 100+ incremental bills to keep the government open but the Senate refused to pass any of these bills until the Republican Party gives a Clean CR and accept Obamacare without any debates or concessions. That is not only a foolish but also a dangerous move. The House Republicans have continued to pass incremental bills to fund military pay flowing, the intelligence community running to protect us around the world, Parks open, Military memorials and basic government offices running including the military accounting office which the Democrats may let pass in the Senate.

ACA now called the Un-Affordable care was created and pushed into law without any debate or bi-partisan support and is now creating problems so vast throughout the United States economically that people are angry, frustrated and scared. The USA is a Democratic nation and compromise is an essential part of running a country built on democracy. We cannot afford to go off on our own without a forum of debates or speaking with both sides of the aisle.

What President Obama meant to do is very commendable but in reality he has harmed his position. He said he would have bi-partisan debates and speak with House Republicans and at the same time he was circumventing them to get this bill put into law without any republican support. It may be that President Obama might have meant that he was willing to talk with the Republican Party after the law went into effect but this is not the proper manner in which to get bi-partisan support from the Republican Party.

He is now playing hardball again but we need to stop the rhetoric and get back to the table. The ACA or as the republican party is now calling Obamacare the Un-affordable Care Act. We need to re-instate former policies so all Americans can continue to be treated correctly and get back to their lives. President Obama has also created 20 new taxes that all Americans will be forced to pay
starting on January 1, 2014. These 20 new taxes were setup by the Democratic Party to make the American people pay for Obamacare and force their hand. The Democrats knew that by creating the Employer mandate the corporations in this country were going to find another way to

avoid paying for benefits and insurance if possible. The Democrats were going to need another way to pay for Obamacare if the monies were not there from the employers and the people. How could the Democrats continue to afford Obamacare-ACA even if there are no other monies to fund it?

Create additional taxes that will further increase spending levels and keep it funded even after the President's term in office is over. What does this mean? It means the non-profits and for-profits were trying to decide how to get out of paying for additional costs of doing business. The ACA was now going to put a strangle-hold on businesses and non-profits across the USA and they needed to figure out how to stay in compliance while maintaining their budgets. This is why creating 20 new taxes would continue to help fund the ACA long after they are gone.

The American people are going to be very angry once these 20 new taxes are implemented in January 2014. This is why President Obama realized that he needed to extend the Employer Mandate from being implemented for another year. Employers were not going to be ready for the mandate and in order to give corporations enough time to prepare for these mandates President Obama made changes to that portion of the ACA to reflect that employers would not have to implement the changes for another year. In the meantime employers have been cutting hours or eliminating jobs to avoid paying the benefits and insurance. In this way employers will continue to increase their bottom-line and find new ways to avoid paying for more insurance which will also cripple those companies future income.

Some of the non-profits and for-profits eliminated the jobs that people were doing without the insurance and benefits. Other entities have just cut the hours of their workers to avoid paying for the insurance and health care that the ACA or Affordable Care Act was supposed to help.

It is an unfortunate consequence but it is resolvable. With some minor changes in the ACA or Affordable Care Act the wording should be replaced so it can be interpreted that if a person who is an hourly staff member and works for a set amount of time above normal hours such as 55+ hours will be allowed to have a portion or percentage of their affordable care and benefits paid for by the employer.

The United States has always been a country of volunteers. If we set the ACA wording that US citizens can opt to voluntarily join the ACA and switch their health care coverage than more people would probably sign up for the ACA. If we do not have a choice then we will feel obligated to again fight for our right of choice.

This is a country that fought and won our freedom from English rule and tyranny to fight for freedom of choice. freedom of religion, freedom to speak, freedom to seek Life, Liberty and the pursuit of

Happiness.

Why are we now being told that we are not allowed to disagree, we are not allowed any choice and if we do not follow this demand we will be fined for not following the law? This is another kind of tyranny and this presidency may find that America is not ready to be pushed into taking something that is ultimately bad for us. This is probably why President Obama also made sure he setup another budget for the IRS of another 500 million dollars to make sure that the people who are being fined will pay those fines and the IRS will become the watchdog to make sure everyone is paying what is owed.

If the American people and other elected officials feel that the country is being misled, we have lost our trust in the President or he has lied to the American people such as saying our insurance rates would go down and we would not have to lose our providers. It is possible that he has misused his duties and authority over the American people and this could open the door or lead to impeachment proceedings.

What is sad is that President Obama had a very high ideal and meant to help the people of the United States of America. He nor the Democratic Party are responsible for the decisions made by businesses and entities that are looking to circumvent the laws of the United States of America. His work with those in the Senate and the House can use this as a win-win scenario if both sides are willing to make some concessions and compromises so that all Americans can still be provided voluntary affordable health care. It is a no win scenario to continue to stonewall the Republican Party or even attempt to demonize their efforts in the House of Representatives. To reiterate the Republican Party passed over 100+ incremental bills in the House and then sent them to the floor of the Senate.

The Republican Party worked tirelessly to open up the government and could continue to run in some small measures at least. We need the Senate majority and the House majority to cross party lines and agree to talk about where we are in the government shutdown and what needs to take place to move forward. Even if in some small measure we are able to talk with one another then we can resolve some of the minor issues that are keeping us from going forward. It was well documented during the last shutdown during the Clinton Administration that he was in daily contact with Republican leaders to find a resolution to the government shutdown.

Now that the Republican leadership gave a Clean CR and the U.S. Government opened back up for business the Democrats in the House and the Senate are starting to realize that they need to work with their counterparts in the House and the Senate and disagree openly with the President of the United States if they are going to have another term in the

House or the Senate. It is not in the best interests of the Democrats to continue to agree with the President now that the government is open again for business. The American people know that the Democrats did nothing and simply kowtowed when they had an opportunity to stand up for what was right. Representative Pelosi and Senator Reid in particular made sure that Democrats in the Senate continued to keep silent when they had an opportunity to speak up and protect the rights of the people or respond to the Republicans and identifying that what the rest of the Democrats were doing was not only wrong but political suicide to their careers.

More than 39 Democrats crossed the line the moment the U.S. Government opened back up for business stating that they agree with Republican leadership that President Obama and his Administration had gone too far and they were willing to work with the Republicans in the House and the Senate to make necessary changes to the policies and make sure we do not default on our debt ceiling, make changes to the sequestration and work to solve the problems with the ACA. This was a welcome sight to millions of people when we started reading it in the newspapers.

10 PRESIDENTIAL MOTIVATIONS

This is not a book looking to psychoanalyze the political decision-makers. We cannot possibly understand all of the factors involved as policy leaders must take into account as they all will contribute to the decision paradigm. The levels of stress, deprivation of sleep, pressures involved at the national and international levels increase as time continues to pass. Some leaders rise to the challenges while others have mental breakdowns.

This independent perspective can only take into account superficially what areas are at stake as political directions are strained within the confines of these new policies, mandates and laws. We can only speculate as to the effects these policies will have upon the citizens of the United States of America as they begin to be implemented. There really is no scenario or political landscape that we can use to evaluate the effect of these new policies. The policies are going to have wide-spread problems throughout the United States unless we are able to relieve much of the pressure by rewriting policy, repealing portions of the law that may harm the American people and work to fix the problems before they shutdown other systems that may be critical to the infrastructure of the United States of America.

The President refusing to speak with Republican leaders and continue stonewalling until his demands were met is indicative of a diplomatic strategy in building psychological support in collaborative efforts of presidential decision-makers. One of the newest strategies that might be used to change the political decision making landscape is a strategy of using multiple devil's advocates to create a dissenting view but this is not effective in most circumstances due to one person having to role-play in using this argumentative strategy. A more elegant solution in simulating the devil's advocate role to assist presidential decisions in complex organizations is to structure scenarios using multiple devil's advocates.

In this manner the role-playing creates another dimension that assists the decision making process by creating strength using multiple role-players or devil's advocates. This is similar to multiple advisors creating solutions that had never been attempted while at the same time they can build in a more elaborate analysis while reducing hierarchical distortion of the policy process.

In President Obama's view this could harm his legacy and promises to the American people. Let us look at it in another way. Do you want to stick to your guns even if the American people you are trying to help are the same American people who cannot afford to lose any of their work hours or their jobs and are possibly losing both. If the American people can no longer afford to pay their bills clearly this will not end well. By simply maneuvering in such a way that the President wants to work with medical and business advisors in order to reword some of the ACA or Affordable Care Act to include wording that all people will be given the opportunity to volunteer for discounts on their medications and benefits depending on their annual income this would make more sense.

The average middle-class worker today works somewhere between 60 and 90 hours a week. They will be unaffected by the changes in the ACA but making them take insurance they do not need and premiums they do not want to pay will be untenable.

The workers that are putting in 40 hours a week or less are the people who will be affected the most by President Obama's ACA. These are the people who voted him into office. The only reason I can think of as to why President Obama would have targeted the people who voted for him was due to a lack of knowledge or wording of the Obamacare. He must be completely unaware of the wording of the 2,572 pages of ACA and what affect that wording is having on the Democratic voters and his constituents. It is unfortunate that the people who are being hurt by the ACA will only be able to interpret this in a few ways. Either President Obama knows he is destroying the people who voted for him, he is unaware of what affect the Affordable Care Act is having on the American people or someone else is pulling the strings and President Obama has not been in control of his presidency.

There is another way the Republicans could work with the Democrats to change the wording of the ACA that might create a win-win scenario. If the American people were given a discount depending on their annual incomes this would instantly become a win-win scenario and it is the smart thing to do. If the Democrats on the hill continue to stonewall the Republican Party it may not be possible to have future negotiations due to the lack of trust from both sides of the aisle.

It is imperative that the Democrats and the Republicans start to share the true ramifications concerning what this means for the American people. Businesses in every state are cutting the hours of workers and making it impossible to survive this undue hardship. This is not happening on one side of the USA or in one town or one state. This is being felt on a national level and in every state in the United States of America.

The effects economically are so vast and widespread that this will ultimately destroy the middle class and close small businesses all across the nation who will not be able to remain solvent in this new economic storm. If the Republican party is not allowed to continue to pass incremental bills that may help President Obama's government to open up slowly than the people of the United States are going to start to lay blame directly upon the President of the United States. There is no need for President Obama to take upon himself all the blame when someone else drafted the ACA.

If your own advisors tell you that the wording is not correct and you do not heed their advice or you fail to fix these issues and refuse to work with Republican Party leadership to resolve these issues then this will cause many more problems. If however the President's own advisors never bothered to point out what was wrong with Obamacare then someone clearly dropped the ball. Ultimately the buck does stop with the President of the United States and yet at the same time there should have been enough leadership within the invisible counsel of advisors to straighten this out and step up to the plate to do the right thing and tell the President that something was missing.

The whole idea of having and inner cabinet of advisors that can keep the President advised of what is transpiring within his presidency is absolutely essential. It cannot be overstated how serious it is to have people within the President's cabinet that will not let him be blind-sided by something as important than the legislation he has set his presidency fulfilling.

11 BARGAINING CHIPS

The Democrat Senator Harry Reid, Majority Leader from Nevada sees the Clean Continuing Resolution as nothing more than a bargaining chip. Senator Reid and Democratic Representative Nancy Pelosi have been stonewalling the Republican party until the Republicans let all of the Government open up and accept Obamacre without any concessions whatsoever. The Democrats are using these photo Ops to point out that it is the Republican Party that is responsible for these funding debacles.

Senator Reid has stated during every Photo Op that he is willing to talk about anything with Republican leadership and Congressman Boehner. Senator Reid stated emphatically "The Democratic Party will not budge on the ACA, this is President Obama's Invisible Counsel telling Senator Reid and Representative Pelosi to blame Republicans in the House and the Senate.

Once the House Republicans get enough of the incremental bills passed they are sent to the Senate. The Senate refused to pass any of the incremental bills due to rhetoric that President Obama wants pushed forward without reservations. The Democrats waited for the Republicans to talk about whatever they wanted to talk about even though they know Democrats will not talk about anything until the Clean CR has been given without objection or concessions.

The Democrats talked about a lack of communication but they must be referring to themselves. The Republicans have been asking for talks since October 1st but the Senate is following the leadership of Senator Reid and House Democrats are following Representative Pelosi who are staying firm on what Obama is calling the Republican's shutdown.

It is clear that the Democrats closed down the Government in order to get the Clean CR which the Republicans can no longer give. The Democrats and the President are using these problems to blame the House and to demon-ize the Republican efforts to get their 100+ incremental bills passed in the House. Once passed in the House they are sent to the Senate floor who refuse to let any of the bills pass.

The Democrats are saying that they are willing to negotiate but they have all refused to pass any of the incremental bills which have already been passed in the House to keep the government open. Recently the Senate has started passing the incremental bills that have been sent by the Republicans in the House. President Obama has slowly taken his time to pick which bills he will let pass in the Senate so he can show the people that he still controls the U.S. Government.

Democrats see these changes in communication as a waste of their time. The Democrats are saying that it is all the fault of the Republican Party. The Democrats are trying to tell the Republicans what they need to do if they want to communicate with them but this is just another way to stonewall the Republican Party leadership. The Democrats may have created the ACA but none of the leadership of the Democratic Party are signing up for it and are in point of fact exempt from signing up for it. The Democrats say they are happy to talk with the House Republicans but they are simply using their rhetoric as leverage against the Republican Party and holding the people of the United States and our debt-ceiling hostage.

The President does not have to sign up for Obamacare and neither does the House of Representatives or the U.S. Senate. If the ACA is so great for the American people why are U.S. leaders not signing up for it? Could it be that it is not as good as the Democrats say it is and if they love the Obamacare then why wasn't the President of the United States the first one to sign up for it?

Democratic Senator Tom Udall of New Mexico stated that "we should have a serious budget, we should reform the middle class and help to take care of our seniors, we still should be talking with the Republican Party majority. We are lurching from crisis to crisis and self-inflicted wounds. The American people want to not lose the American dream and the people are scared and frustrated about their futures." Senator Udall is exactly right and he along with Senator Franken were some of the few Democratic Party members to stand up and speak about how the ACA is going to ruin the future of the American people right in the middle of the Government shutdown. Senator Franken and Senator Udall men of character willing to stand up and speak for their constituents.

They are not wrong we need a budget but the middle-class doesn't need reform. The middle-class voted you into office and without them you would not even be in office. Democratic Senator Udall is not entirely correct, the political debates and the Democratic and Republican Party are needing to get together and back to the table.

The Senate has not created a single budget, not one. If the Republican Party wants to show how important it is to gain concessions concerning the ACA, I believe they have done it. The Democratic Party is making no concessions which means that although the Republican Party wants to open up the government and has passed several bills in the House to open up government the Senate continued to refuse to even vote on any of the bills sent to them by the Republicans in the House.

The Senate majority had been trying to pass the smaller bills that the House majority had sent to the Senate but the Democratic leadership continued to stop the bills from passing in the Senate. We were not able to get the Democratic party to even show up to meet and speak about opening the government.

Congressman Boehner stated to the media and the floor of the House "We are not going to let our Sovereign debt fail." If we want to be fiscally responsible we need to take baby steps to pass these incremental bills that will slowly open the government up again and get it running. Again Congressman Boehner "Why have the Democrats been holding the parks, the military, the intelligence community, and the DOD transportation hostage by **not** letting them go to work or get paid until government is turned back on?" Why is it that President Obama has added some 1100 special interest groups to be funded when it is clear that we are getting dangerously too close to our debt ceiling? Why try to fund special interest groups at all when we do not have the money to fund it. We needed to start paying our debt back.

The Democratic party held many of these necessary government institutions hostage and closed until they decided to pass the incremental bills at a point when it would be clear that the Democrats were in charge of fixing the shutdown. It is obvious that President Obama is running the Senate and in particular which bills he was going let pass through the Senate so President Obama could show his ability to lead. They did not let any important programs turn back on till the Republican Party gave the Clean CR and funded the rest of Obamacare without any concessions. This is tyrannical to say the least and no one should be bullied in the USA to join a program they cannot afford for a health insurance they do not need.

What is strange is at the same time the government was shut down the Democrats also shut down the Intelligence Community. Military logistics including being able to transport people, materials, supplies and fuel for military operations were also automatically shut down by sequestration while the government was shutdown. Leaders on both sides of the aisle were flabbergasted by this maneuvering by the President to use sequestration as a pawn in the struggle to gain the Clean CR from the Republicans in the House of Representatives while putting the country at risk.

To put the entire country at risk to its' enemies and using our men and women in our Armed Forces as pawns in a deadly game of political maneuvering and sandbagging to win what the president believes to be the most important part of the shutdown battle to make sure he is given his Clean Continuing Resolution is one of the most dangerous games I have ever seen conducted on Capitol Hill.

President Obama must have told the Democratic leadership in the Senate that he wanted nothing to be signed until he was given the Clean CR by House Republicans. He finally decided to let the Senate pass some of the incremental bills sent to the Senate by the House of Representatives at the end of September and through mid-October. The bills passed by the House were sent to the Senate but the Democrats in the Senate were not allowed to cross Party lines and vote for any of the incremental bills unless given the OK by Senator Reid or Representative Pelosi. President Obama was stonewalling the Republican Party leadership and at the same time he was putting us all at risk for several days while the military was not being paid, the intelligence community was sent home, military logistics including the transports for moving materials, people and fuel were no longer active which means it placed undue risk on the United States of America and our soldiers around the world.

The President of the United States of America was only weakening this country at the expense of the Clean CR and blaming it all on the Republicans in the House of Representatives. We cannot afford to continue to avoid this stalemate and we need to be good and fair to the American people and do the right thing and deal with the problems that are necessary to take care of right now. At the same time we do not want to give any concessions to leaders in the Senate or the House dealing with the Un-Affordable Care Act.

The Republican party has been working to get the Democrats back to the table. What is painfully obvious is that President Obama is not trying to get back to the table. President Obama has been listening to his advisors but for some reason they have no breathing room and can offer no alternatives to solve this problem. If the President's advisors had any other solutions they would have at least maneuvered into a position of strength before refusing to talk with Party Republicans. This in my opinion is a clear sign that even though President Obama has been steadily maneuvering he decided to place all of the responsibility directly upon the Republicans even though the Democrats are following President Obama's directions and took a very long time before starting to pass any of the incremental bills sent to the Senate by the House of Representatives.

The Republican Party majority and Tea Party were voted into office in the Senate and the House of Representatives to shut down the ACA or un-Affordable Care Act. It is their bread and butter and they are not going to back down unless the Democratic Party starts to give concessions in order to open a portion of the US Government. If they did not get some of their concessions the Republican Party would have continued to keep passing and sending additional incremental bills to the floor of the Senate.

It is the elite of the Democratic Party that stonewalled the Republican Party but make no mistake about this they are not alone. The Republican Party elite are also summarily holding back from letting the government open up entirely. They saw the Coercive Diplomacy during these maneuvering strategies by President Obama and were more than willing to let the president stall in the Whitehouse. The Republican Party moderates in the Senate and the House could not change the direction of the Tea Party elite.

Many Republicans in the House and the Senate recognized that Obamacare or the Un-Affordable Care Act should never have been allowed to continue. The American people are going to have a voice and will bring up these issues at the next election. Using the Sovereign Debt as an avenue to push for concessions on Obamacare was a no-win scenario. The average person in the United States of America recognizes that the Tea Party is trying to protect our civil liberties and our rights to choose not to select the ACA. We need our Democrats in the Senate, our Republicans in the House to step up to the plate and stand up for the rights of working men and women in this country.

What President Obama wanted to do to protect the American people and provide affordable care is an important need. President Obama's invisible counsel have seriously placed him in a very bad light. In principal his legislation was a huge step forward but in practicality it was an utterly monster or huge failure. Not only can it not go forward as it is written, it will need to be completely over-hauled if it will ever be implemented. If moderate Republicans can convince moderate Democrats that they will work to help fix the ACA to make it truly affordable to low income individuals in a fully bi-partisan process then the Obama Administration may let some concessions be placed within the legislation of the ACA.

It is imperative to President Obama that he not lose face over the fulcrum of his legacy which stems from his work on the ACA. Instead of de-funding or eliminating the ACA completely it would be wise to work to convince President Obama and his Administration that the Republicans understand that he was simply trying to help the American people and to offer them something that has never been done before a medical coverage that is affordable.

I am convinced as we watched President Obama maneuver and sandbag the Republican Party leadership that stalling his requests were not going to bring about the outcome the Tea Party had anticipated. Working with President Obama to assist him and provide a good, sound, and fair legislation for the entire population of the United States of America is an essential first step in the process of fixing the ACA. Making it voluntary once it is fixed will convince Americans to sign up for it.

This bi-partisan group will need to add wording to reflect that once workers are putting in 60 hours or more they will automatically be allowed benefits and insurance. It is imperative that hard working hourly Americans not have their hours cut to 28 per week which is a loss of 48 hours per month and 600 hours of lost pay per year. This has now cut their pay annually by 30% per year.

Senator Al Franken from Minnesota shared in the middle of the shutdown on the floor of the Senate that people in Minnesota are hurting. They are not sure if they will be able to pay their bills, their mortgages and they need their hours and their pay back at the levels they were before the ACA kicked off. Senator Franken is a voice of reason and is smart enough to realize that the ACA is not going to work the way it is presently written. He is a moderate Democrat who really wants to work on this process that will make this legislation affordable for his constituents and all Americans.

It is the ACA that the Republican Party wants to add concessions to in order to stop the American people from losing 48+ hours from their paychecks each month. We must get those hours back and at the same time repeal or fix the wording of the ACA in a bi-partisan committee. How can this be? This became effective the moment the ACA or Affordable Care Act became a law. Again this is caused by the "miss-wording," of the ACA which is interpreted as if an hourly person in the USA works for more than 30 hours per week they are entitled to insurance and benefits. Why didn't the ACA just say that all persons who work hourly more than 60 hours per week automatically get insurance and benefits. If this were the case then the hours lost would have been minimal to each person but instead this law is now summarily destroying the hourly working class and anyone who believes in the American dream.

The country needs to realize that we are all in the same boat. This is no longer about Democrats or Republicans, this is about everyone who works in this country. It does not matter what your ideology is or what party you voted for in the last election. This is all about people losing their jobs, all people putting food on the table, all people paying their bills. If you think this is not going to affect you because you have a full time job you are going to be mistaken. Sooner or later the employer mandate will give employers an opportunity to eliminate insurance for all workers. Once this happens everyone will feel the crunch.

The ACA is only the tip of the iceberg. With the Debt-Ceiling that must be amended and looming over us we also need to curtail sequestration. It also needs to be fixed to not include critical and logistical programs related to all Intelligence agencies including but not limited to the following: GSI, CIA, NSA, Military and SPECOPS commands from all branches that may be creating havoc as it automatically shuts down programs. These also include U.S. Military programs, logistics, government programs, social security programs, military pay, scientific and research programs such as the National Science Foundation, as well as NASA that rely heavily on funding from the Federal government must remain open and could cause unanticipated problems that could put our country and our soldiers at risk around the world.

It is imperative that some programs should never be shutdown such as the intelligence community, military transports that move troops from one base to another anywhere in the world, military logistics, refueling planes that keep our military in the air, supplies, weapons and food. I am certain our Democratic and Republican Parties are recognizing that the American people will need their help before the Affordable Care Act will be changed effectively for the people in the USA.

12 LESSONS FROM THE PAST

Let us learn from the mistakes of the past: In the mid-1990's the contractors who worked for Microsoft decided they wanted insurance and benefits so they sued Microsoft in court. Guess what? The contractors won in court and were allowed to have insurance and benefits if they had worked for more than 18 months as a contractor.

What did big business do next to circumvent the law and save on their bottom line? Yes, Microsoft and every company in the United States of America that had contractors for more than 18 months immediately fired all their contractors. I know that this happened just this way. How do I know about it? I was an Information Technology contractor during this time and my contract was not supposed to end for another five years. My contract ended after 18 months and I was not exactly thrilled by the prospect that this was caused by a few people who wanted benefits by their contracting employer. Once it became a law it didn't just affect Microsoft but every company in the United States of America. In the long-run the contractors all lost their contracts and according to the rule of that law the contractor was not allowed to be hired for at least a year or the company would have to give the contractors the insurance and benefits they were due. Just because something is passed into law does not necessarily make it a sound solution.

Being a law may make it the law of the land but that doesn't mean the law is drawn up perfectly and can't be changed. Just because it becomes a law does not mean it shouldn't be repealed and changed into something that will work for citizens. Let us not throw away the good that the ACA law is providing but simply change it to reflect the necessities and the provisions that are necessary to protect the insurance and benefits that are needed.

Let's change the ACA to reflect that all contractors, hourly staff, part-time workers and freelance workers can have the insurance and benefits if they work 60 hours or more per week. Do not take the hours that they do work, all you have to do is add the hours that their employer would need them to work in order to be allowed to get the insurance and benefits.

This would immediately solve 2 problems. The people who already work full time would continue to get their insurance and benefits and the people who were making contractors, hourly staff, part-timers and freelance workers work longer hours would no longer be allowed to use them beyond normal business hours of 40 hours without paying them additional wages, insurance and benefits.

This is not brain-surgery. We simply need to treat people correctly and provide for them if they are providing extra hours for companies. It is a matter of basic principal and fair labor. It is a simple matter of retrieving the portions of the Affordable Care Act that do not make sense and do not force businesses to provide insurance to workers that they cannot afford.

All laws have additional changes when they no longer make sense and many dollars have been rescinded after laws have been passed when the funding limits were identified as being too high. President Obama rescinded many of the dollars that seemed too high in the middle of the Summer of 2012.

This is certainly true of the Medical Device Tax since it was repealed on the Senate floor by the majority of the Democrats after it was found to be too costly for patients. Why is this a different set of circumstances and why do the Democrats refuse to negotiate? A plausible reason why the Democratic elite have refused to come to the table and discuss the issues surrounding Obamacare which it is now being called has to do with the next election in 2016.

In order to elect another Democratic President it is necessary to damage the reputation of the existing Republican Party while effectively appearing more powerful before the people. Although I have heard this view I do not believe it holds much merit. However I have watched the Democrats including Senator Harry Reid and Representative Nancy Pelosi hurl insults and resort to name calling towards Republican Party leaders who are simply trying to meet with the President and Senate Democratic leaders to discuss these very important issues. We simply need to add additional information to the provisions to provide additional insurance and benefits for workers who qualify.

If we do not fix the ACA law now, the 17 Trillion dollar deficit will increase exponentially due to a further slowed economy caused by more people who will not be able to pay their bills, mortgages and double or triple rising insurance premiums because the ACA will force businesses to cut the hours of their employees so it stays below the 30 hours outlined in the ACA.

Republican from New Hampshire Senator Kelly Ayotte spoke on the Senate floor and I quote, " I have constituents who voted for Obamacare because they were told they were allowed to keep their doctors and now that it is a law they found out that this turned out to be a lie."

She voted to repeal the medical device tax which was found to further increase medical costs and when the vote was completed it was 79 to 20 to repeal it and it is no longer a part of Obamacare.

Senator Ayotte is not the only Senator that has heard from their constituents concerning losing their doctors. Having to take a different Health Provider even though they were happy with their health care and now being told they have to have something else again and they have to pay a great deal more for it is a disaster.

Why has the Clean CR become such a hot topic at the same time President Obama and the Democratic Senate continue to stall incremental bills from the House that would open the US Government? In making decisions the President of the United States must have a clear picture of any changes in policy that may affect strategic decisions toward any future implementations. Therefore it is imperative that President Obama keep well informed by using advisors for any and all needs. It must have been the President's advisors that identified the best time in which to write a new law and when would be the best time to send it to the floor of the Senate with the least amount of objection. Ultimately the buck does stop at the desk of the oval office.

President Obama has been using his close advisors to play hardball and by continuing to use a tactic where he uses multiple-Devil's advocates to arrive at a solution that will keep him informed and in a position of strength while continually keeping the Republicans in the House at bay. If this is not the case then why has President Obama avoided speaking with Republican Party leadership until only recently? All Presidents have a very small select group of advisors who are either outside the party or are within his own cabinet that keep him apprised of all possible analytical theories and scenarios that may redirect the political players to his advantage. It is very Presidential for the president to use his advisors to strategically theorize what would be the best decision in implementing new policy and submitting new resolutions without objections.

There is a small contingent of elite Democrats in the Senate that would rather stalemate the issues of ACA, Clean CR, the Debt-Ceiling and keeping government open by undermining any negotiations from taking place. It is their contention that the longer a stalemate takes place the more blame will be dumped onto the Republican Party in the House of Representatives.

This is simply not what is actually happening in the Senate. The Democratic Majority Leader Senator Harry Reid and Representative Nancy Pelosi are identifying to party members how they want them to vote in order to get a stronger bargaining chip into the hands of President Obama so his policies can move forward without any opposition. The problem with this possible scenario is that the Democrats in the Senate could find themselves bumped out of office at the next election because they stalled in the Senate while their constituents were calling and writing and wanting to know why they are not being served.

Why did none of the Senate move forward when the House Republicans were sending over 100 incremental bills passed on the floor of the House to the Senate? Why didn't even 1 Democratic Senator speak out about needing to walk across the aisle to get a deal setup? Why did the Democrats just sit on their hands while the Republicans in the House continually passed and sent incremental bills from the House to the floor of the Senate to open up the Government?

Is it because the Senate leader Reid had complete control over the Senate and wanted to put all the power directly in the hands of the President of the United States? The Democrats in the Senate are going to follow party lines and Senate leadership to continue to appear strong. In reality the Democrats are bringing attention to the fact that their own party is blindly following the Democratic Elite rhetoric.

Democratic Party leadership have already identified the process by which they will go forward to force the Republican Party to relinquish the remaining authority that resides within the framework of the Clean CR. President Obama has stopped communicating with the Republican Party leadership and instead is very slowly selecting which incremental bills he is going to select from the House of Representatives and he will let pass in the Senate to show how strong his position is within the Democratic Party. The President's goal is to force Republican leadership's hand by using Senator Reid and Representative Pelosi to keep the Democrats in line and follow their party to vote only on the measures that will help them to appear in charge of this country.

What is odd is that most people realize that this is nothing more than basic political maneuvering. Using every opportunity to speak with the media and say how they have given every opportunity to the Republicans and their party leadership to come to conference and talk about whatever they want to discuss. The House Republicans have spoken to the media and on the floor of the House to share with the American people that the President of the United States has made no attempts and has no intention of negotiating on any topics at all unless he gets his way. The Clean CR has pieces of legislation that directly affect Obamacare. He is not interested in talking or debating any of Obamacare with Republicans until after they relinquish and give up the Clean CR.

Most people in the United States are unaware that there are pieces of the Clean CR which are directly responsible for the Obamacare framework and it is needed by the Democrats in order to continue to fund it. This is why President Obama demanded it first before he would negotiate. We have observed, Senator Reid and Rep. Pelosi are Democratic Evangelists who believe that all the problems with this country are the fault of the Republican Party. Using basic common sense I would say it takes two to tango and there is no way any one party can possibly be at fault for the woes of this administration.

Reid and Pelosi are both hard line Democrats and I would venture to say they would not do anything without President Obama's say so. His Invisible Counsel or close party advisors have convinced him that the tack he is using presently is the only clear way in which to force the Republicans to give a Clean CR. Senator Reid and Rep. Pelosi are using every opportunity to speak with the media to demon-ize the Republican Party by blaming them for what history will identify as a law that was pushed onto the American people by the Democratic Party and in no small part by the President of the United States. The President's advisors must have come to the realization that the only way to diminish all the responsibility falling directly upon the Democratic party was to wait long enough so that the bulls-eye is now on all political players instead of only a single party.

The Democratic elite have tried on at least seven occasions to blame this stalemate on Congressman John Boehner and the Republican Party even though it is not House Republican Leadership or even Moderate Republicans that is refusing to speak about Obamacare, Clean CR, the Debt-Ceiling or keeping the US Government open.

This is squarely the responsibility of the President of the United States who was trying to put a strangle-hold on the Republican Party to give a Clean CR to Obamacare even though the entire country no longer wants anything to do with it

The American people have not resorted to it yet but they are allowed to setup a grassroots effort to defund Obamacare by having every person in every town and city and state to call their Congressman, Senators, and political party directly to demand a change in this ACA to reflect the need to protect American workers hours and pay and completely stop Obamacare before it causes any more problems upon the American people.

President Obama must pay his bills and that includes the promises he made to those who paid for his campaign run presidency. If we were to take a look at President Obama's wife for a moment and think about what industry she was working for prior to her husband's bid to become President of the United States we might start to theorize who paid for this campaign.

Clearly the Pharmaceutical Industry and insurance companies have very deep pockets and can pay for such a run for the Oval Office. There is nothing wrong with getting funding from corporate entities and individuals that believe in the candidates.

A perfect example is the Oil Industry and Military manufacturers that supported President Bush Senior and President Bush Junior as they took their run for the Whitehouse. What can be disturbing is what length or tack will a President decide to take in order to repay his corporate supporters who may have bank-rolled his campaigns? It really depends on what promises were made to ensure continued generosity remains available in providing the springboard to keep a president in the Oval Office for two terms.

13 WHAT NEEDS TO BE DONE ?

Sequestration should never have been setup for any critical programs that protect the United States of America. It should not be shutting down programs that run the utilities that keep our infrastructure running and our people supplied with power, electricity, and water. It should not affect our intelligence programs and operations around the world from running and protecting our country. In my opinion it should not be running at all. Why should it not be running?

To those who do not understand what sequestration is in simple terms, it is an automatic turning off of programs in order to stop us from going beyond our debts. It was put in place to stop programs automatically. It should never have been put in motion to shut down programs without giving the people in charge of running this country an opportunity to speak on behalf of those programs and make the hard decisions to keep some running and some not running.

It is the responsibility of the Executive Branch, the Senate and the House to debate, to meet in sessions, to go to committees to bring about what is needed and what is not needed. To write bills and vote on what should be in place and what should not be put in place to protect this country for our children's children' s children.

We have a serious amount of work to accomplish and it is our sovereign right to come to office and follow procedures set in place by the Constitution of the United States and the Declaration of Independence using proper procedures and Robert's Rules of Order to take the correct steps in arriving at important decisions through the use of checks and balances.

We do not want anyone to create a program that takes the decision making process out of the hands of our politically elected officials responsibility. Now that we know that sequestration was a mistake we need to make sure it is turned off and eliminated before it causes any more problems to any of our critical or non-critical programs. If it turns off payments or shuts down financial programs, health programs, Institutional programs that are critical to running this country, critical to running our military, critical to keeping electrical systems, power grids, water and nuclear programs running than it needs to be turned off and shutdown before it weakens our infrastructure or any other part of keeping this country running.

At the same time we need to show our global partners that we are committed to paying back our debts. Even if the current president does nothing but the Republican Party states emphatically to the Press that "We are not going to default on our debt," as Congressman Boehner did so eloquently it is still a win-win for the presidency.

Our global partners and supporters around the world know we are going to pay off these debts. We are not going to default and it shows great resiliency and poise for someone under a great deal of pressure such as Congressman Boehner to speak so candidly to the Press. "

We know that some of these debts were caused by the previous administration but we have been continuing to fund our military overseas in Iraq and Afghanistan when we should have pulled out already and been working to strengthen our country, pay our debts, rebuild from several devastating storms and financial crisis that continue to increase our future indebtedness.

We need to make immediate decisions and show our global partners that we are committed to them. We need to strengthen our ties to our allies and safeguard our friends including Israel. Even when the Republican leadership in the House state to the media and the floor of the House that we are not going to default on our debt it is still a win-win for the Presidency.

However if most people in the United States think for a moment concerning how these internal political changes will affect their bottom line they will realize that all the people can speak as one voice. We need to rethink what is most important to our future. Most people would agree that who we voted for in the last election has almost no bearing on where we go from here. The reason this is true has to do with how we are affected by the Obamacare and what is happening throughout small town America. Small town America in this context refers to every town, county, city and state in the United States of America. This is including our people in Puerto Rico and Guam. They are feeling the same circumstances that are affecting everyone else in the continental United States.

There is a very real and plausible explanation as to why President Obama has not moved forward in working with or talking to Republican leadership. This has to do with his invisible counsel of advisors who normally would be giving both collected, analyzed, real data and the analysis which is critical and crucial as he considers the options, alternatives and possible outcomes that may play out between Party leadership. If President Obama is only using his top advisors and the only real alternative is to stall in order to lay blame upon the other party this will not bode well.

It cannot be over stated how crucial these next six months of negotiations, compromise and proper Presidential maneuvering may be necessary on the part of the President. When assessing risk and vulnerabilities a basic premise of the advisory process is to develop several advisory lines of communication, information collection and analysis in order to build a coordinated and qualified effort that will eliminate excessive complications in order to arrive at a solution that is both simplistic and clear.

There are political makers and takers that do not see any side but their own and whoever is not kowtowing to their agenda is the enemy. This is only a select few that think they are impervious to critical analysis. I would certainly put Senator Reid and Rep. Pelosi into the realm of Democratic Evangelists who were put in charge of getting their people under their control. Sometimes by internal bullying, sometimes by political isolation. They have been given the power by their leadership. Yes, it goes without saying that the highest point in their political landscape in the presidency.

From a purely independent perspective we have to realize that ultimately Rep. Pelosi and Senator Reid would not have said a word unless given the OK by the president himself. They were probably coached by the invisible counsel advisory at the president's right hand. As Democratic leadership from the House and the Senate they are nothing more than puppets whose strings are being manipulated by the president.

His the President's overall goal would be to strengthen the Democratic Party at the same time he was weakening the Republican Party to run the political landscape in America to his overall advantage. Pushing his agenda even to the detriment of his own Party if necessary to make sure his own historical legacy remained in-tact.

Once the Clean CR was given by the Republican leadership to President Obama at the end of October the Democrats in the House and the Senate would have felt distinctly "out in the cold." Realizing they had better be able to jump into a bi-partisan stance so they can be seen by their constituents as men and women willing to work together to resolve the problems with Obamacare, Sequestration, the Debt-Ceiling and the defaulting of our debts. These 39 Democrats immediately began crossing the aisle to avoid the appearance that they were playing hardball with the Republicans in the House and the Senate and show those at home that they want to work to resolve these issues for their constituents. These 39 men and women of the Democratic Party had to make sweeping changes in order to show people back home that they wanted to stay in the House and the Senate.

One of the things used by Senator Reid and Rep. Pelosi was having their own Party use of name calling and resorting to disparaging other leaders with remarks aimed to hurt their integrity just to get under their skin is nothing new. Using it to get a rise out of someone when you disagree with their views has been used many times politically and in amateur and professional sports but in the information age and at a time when our country has failed to protect the American people from laws that would damage their futures and health it is really considered a bit too destructive.

Name calling and trash-talking rivals has been going on for thousands of years. Calling legislators here in America anarchists, terrorists, suicide bombers, and wackos does seem a little over the top. The Democratic elite obviously felt they were going to get a rise out of people calling them names. If the Republicans lashed out after the Democrats called them names they could act overly sensitive and the media could play upon these disparaging remarks.

This is not new but at a time when terrorism has been on the rise for the Democrats to use slanderous remarks towards their rivals in the House of Representatives and to equate members of the Republican Party with people who want to kill Americans seems a bit over the top to say the very least. It was most likely Democratic leadership evangelists such as Rep. Pelosi and Senator Reid that wanted Democrats to speak out and openly insult Republican Party leadership.

Anyone willing to take up the reigns of leadership and stand before the people to do what is right for their constituents should be considered a hero. I would certainly put Democratic Senator Al Franken in that category. He spoke up in the middle of the Senate floor during the government shutdown to share how his constituents were being harmed by this new law. He was willing to stand up for the State of Minnesota at a time when it was unpopular and he was speaking about the needs of his constituents from Minnesota.

The Democrats on the floor of the Senate were hardly speaking at all. Rarely during the government shutdown did Democratic Senators share anything but Senator Franken was going to make sure his constituents were being heard from Washington, D.C. Senators and Congressional leaders in the Capital will often do whatever is necessary to regain accolades in the Senate and the House that may strengthen their position when building brinkmanship.

It takes skin like an elephant to put up with all the disregard for the truth, political rhetoric, half-truth, photo ops, adding spins that you do not even agree with in order to redirect political players from other sides of the aisle. There are times that call for political rivalry when leaders feel forced by others to re-align with their political party in order to gain a foothold in upcoming elections. Votes may sometimes become distant memories that may open avenues for other party members too weak to oppose your position in future debates if your agenda is being re-positioned to align with others.

Political players at times will change their positions to follow Senate or Congressional leadership in their particular Party. This could possibly move you into realms of political positions that may give unintended outcomes and cost you an election even if you disagree. Changing your own positions towards one that will move your opponent to select a different line of control can often mean a disaster in upcoming elections.

This is exactly what has been happening in the Senate and the House during the Government Shutdown. Most of the moderate Democrats in the Senate were not communicating with moderate House Republicans to avoid appearing out of touch with the Democratic leadership elite and to stay in line with Party rhetoric. Senator Reid was using every possible manner to control the Democrats in the Senate so President Obama appeared to be running his Party and keeping control over the country until he got the Clear CR from the Republican leadership. In the end it had little to do with President Obama sandbagging or maneuvering the Democratic Party or his use of coercive diplomacy to control Republicans. The Republicans refused to default on our debt.

14 SUMMARY

What is interesting about this new program of the Affordable Care Act is it was actually started by Hillary Clinton who championed the needs of the people to have affordable health care and she started working on it during former President Bill Clinton's terms in office.

I have no real answers for you but clearly something is amiss when the Federal Government takes measures to create a law that is not protecting the rights of its citizens. The civil liberties are being circumvented and people are told they are <u>not</u> allowed to voluntarily join but must join or be fined. Is it possible that amongst the 2,572 pages of the ACA President Obama has added more than 20 new tax hikes for America to pay in order to fund Obamacare?

Why would he add the taxes to continue to fund Obamacare? It is to make sure everyone who signs up also has to pay for this plan that is going to cost the average family $20,000 dollars a year in health care costs? Of course that doesn't make sense right? It will make sense if you are a new owner of a pharmaceutical company or an insurance company that is going to cash in on Obamacare.

As an Independent thinker I have to question everyone in the Senate that voted for this bill knowing that they never took the time to read all 2,572 pages. Hearing Representative Pelosi talk to the media about how they need to go ahead and sign it into law and then figure out what it all means without knowing what was written in it. Who in their right mind would sign a contract having not first read what it said and have it explained to them by their lawyers? If Representative Pelosi was running a company, the Board of Directors of that company would have fired her the first time she shared her notion of signing contracts without first reading them.

It is amazing to me what goes on in normal political arenas. How can anything get done in an institution that is so far removed from reality? I would like to know who wrote this bill for all the Senators to sign. The Democrats in the Senate have quite possibly made the worst mistake of their political careers by voting for this bill. If it doesn't succeed, now that it's law, the Democratic U.S. Senators will have a hard fight to stay in office during the next election.

If the Un-affordable Care Act doesn't remotely fix those without health care the American people will want to replace the Democrats in the Senate and the House for not standing up for their constituents. The American people are going to want someone like Paul Ryan who has assisted the Democrats as well as the Republican party by creating budgets that make sense. The people are going to be very upset when they find out that there are 20 new tax hikes that will be put in place starting this coming January 1, 2014. They are going to be far more likely to just vote any Republican in office for the next 16 or 20 years and you can bet the Independents, Republicans and the remainder of the Democratic moderates will join forces together to work very hard to reverse every blunder signed into law during your tumultuous administration.

President Obama there has got to be another way to fix this law and still give you your visionary legacy without harming the American people in the process. If the president lets this continue he will have sold the American people out in favor of paying his bills to his supporters. It has been said that the Obamacare website was just one of the companies that funded President Obama's run for the Whitehouse. According to the website only 6 people tried to sign up on the first day and no one succeeded in signing up. No one knows enough about the legislation to even decide if the people have received the right health care coverage.

According to the 2,572 pages of the Un-affordable Care Act every person from the CEO to the janitors will have the same health care coverage. When the rights of American citizens are being thwarted for the rights of all people to have affordable health care they cannot afford and do not need something is clearly wrong.

When I was first told that the Affordable Care Act was approximately 2,572 pages in length it made me think of disinformation. So much documentation that no one would be interested in reading the entire document. Is this what the Democratic leadership intended when they wrote it? Are they making sure they covered every bit of the wording so there would be no chance of misinterpretation? Clearly something was missed in the interpretation of Un-affordable Care Act. Is this the legacy President Obama fought so hard to keep? Is this what 17 trillion dollars pays for? President Obama didn't just sandbag the Republican Party in the House and the Senate, he sandbagged the moderate Democrats in the House and the Senate. He led all the American people not just the Independents, Democrats and Republicans but everyone down a mythical yellow brick road to see the Wizard of Obamacare. There is no wizard to give them courage, intelligence or heart.

So when Senator Reid started bullying the Democrats in the Senate to just agree to vote for the Un-affordable Care Act or else, he got his way. Senator Reid thought he was on the winning side but now he will find out first hand that he was also sold a bill of goods and he will also be fighting for his political career in the next election. President Obama has set his legacy upon his Un-affordable Care Act which is one of the worst legislations ever written. With his demand to implement it even though the HHS or Health and Human Services is still highly vulnerable. HHS is not protecting the private records or social security numbers of private citizens. The HHS has yet to fix the seven separate areas that Mr. David Levinson stated during his testimony on March 19, 2013. Before the United States House of Representatives Committee on Appropriations Subcommittee on Labor, Health and Human Services, Education and Related Agencies at the Rayburn House Office Building in room 2358-C Mr. Levinson gave testimony. With a discretionary budget of $50 million dollars in fiscal year (FY-2012). The Office of Inspector Generals or OIG overseeing 300 Health and Human Services Programs he identified problems that continued to plague Health and Human Services.

Most importantly Mr. Levinson identified deficiencies relating to improperly giving out of Grants, Contracts, misuse of Administration, Data Security vulnerabilities, Improper use of grants, Administration, Emergency preparedness and the Public Health. Since that time the HHS has yet to fix any of these issues. The only thing they have been able to do was to write a plan to implement a process to fix the problems. The plan has never been implemented.

As the leading member of the House of Representatives who only wants to serve honorably and protect the freedoms of the people of the United States of America. Republican Congressman John Boehner of the House of Representatives is a man of great integrity and inner strength. He is very likable by his constituents as well as many people across the U.S. who recognize that he is standing up for the American people and those who cannot stand up for themselves.

What is amazing to me is that Congressman Boehner has not once insulted, resorted to name calling or used any kind of disparaging remarks towards any of the Democratic Party members or the President of the United States. He has come to the oval office on many occasions to speak with the President of the United States and is respected by men and women on both sides of the aisle in both the Senate and the House as a fair and honest man.

He is a man of great character and could be the next president of the United States of America in 2016. Why has it become necessary for Senate and House Democrats to demonize any Republican Party members during this Government Shutdown? That they are trying to get them to conference or resolve these issues is another matter. Could it be due to the need of Democratic leadership to destroy Republican reputations as we head toward the twilight of the Obama Presidency?

This is the first time in US History that a Democratic President wants to keep the government shut down despite members in his own party wanting to cross Democratic Party lines to meet with Republicans in the House to resolve these issues that threaten this economy and may irrevocably destroy the United States of America.

There is a small contingency of elite Democrats in the Senate that would rather stalemate these issues and undermine any negotiations from taking place. Their goal is to force the Republican Party to relinquish the remaining authority that resides within the framework of the Clean CR to add or delete laws to the U-ACA or Obamacare.

The reason it is absolutely necessary for the President of the United States to have the Clean CR is in order for President Obama to receive the rest of the provisions of ACA or the Un-Affordable Care Act. Without any consensus from the Republicans in the House or the Senate. This has been quite unusual considering the Senate majority of Democrats know that the majority of the Republicans in the House are only trying to provide basic rights for the American people.

Another of President Obama's legacies is the Sequestration that should never include critical utilities, Intelligence gathering programs and military logistic needs of fuel, supplies and transportation or government programs that are helping the poor or stopping checks to military members and their families, veterans retirement checks or Social Security checks. Yes, we realize that President Obama is not entirely responsible for the NSA listening in on United States citizens and our allies.

This is nothing new and you can bet that every other country and our allies have been listening to everyone else's communications since World War II. It goes without saying that every country in the world has the right to protect itself and its people. However at the same time the buck does stop with the President of the United States of America. Whether President Obama has full deniability or not he is in charge of this country and as Commander in Chief he must take responsibility for the actions of those in his command and their subordinates. If the NSA or any other programs or agencies were doing something overtly you can bet the President of the United States was also aware of it.

President Obama was not only aware of what these agencies are doing but he is not afraid to share his willingness to tell the intelligence gathering to continue. He wants to know what if any are the other dignitaries talking about before any negotiations can take place here in the United States of America. Someone shared that we are using all the means at our disposal to protect the USA and be vigilant, this is a wise course of action. It is clearly relevant to everyone else in the world that every country is obligated to use whatever means at their disposal to protect themselves. It is not that our allies are upset now concerning wiki-leaks.

They have always known that the NSA has been spying on them all these years just as we have let them spy on us. If other countries do not make a fuss over these wiki-leaks regarding the NSA then allies and foes alike will know that these other global leaders also have the same Telecom capabilities. Our allies and World leaders will demand that we identify why we've continued spying on them all these years since the end of world war II. Most countries use any number of segmented or compartmentalized knowledge in order to have some form of deniability when they are asked direct and compromising questions by their governments.

Having the ability to deny involvement or knowledge regarding areas outside the diplomatic arena keeps countries from crossing the line and having to answer questions. Leaders within actor states utilize areas outside government intervention and at times cross into the grey latitudes of questionable criminal intent to accomplish results outside of bureaucratic influences.

Presidential decision-making motives are sometimes derailed in favor of finishing their goals which are tenuously tied to their agendas. They might opt to cut corners depending on the amount of time remaining as they reach the twilight of their terms in office and solidify their legacy at the expense of their reputation. Not every president finishes their terms in office with all their work accomplished. With Obamacare, the debt ceiling, defaulting on enormous loans and problems with sequestration we need to either support the president or work to fix the problems associated with his presidency.

Remaining independent in my perspective we need to realize that President Obama probably spent his first four years trying to straighten the problems from another presidential legacy. We need to recognize that President Obama had to deal with enormous stress from all our allies, from the problems here at home financially that he had to work to straighten out with the assistance of the Republican Party, the media, from within the Democratic Party moderates and elite.

The Office of the President of the United States is an enormous responsibility and being the leader of the free world often does not come without huge amounts of stress and consequences. No one can possibly know the pressure involved in working night and day for 2920 days in office for a President with two terms. We cannot understand what he must go through to advance his efforts to help the people of the United States of America. No one can possibly fathom the astronomical importance of each and every session, committee or meeting he must attend.

People are wanting to hear President Obama's opinion and desire to

make things work here in the United States. His legacy has to resolve issues and provide a stronger future for his children's children' s children. This cannot be completed without the help of many advisors.   Looking
through the data collected for the day to day operations and the meta-data that is constantly gathered as the president has to make policy decisions. His advisors have to determine which information is relevant, what kind of statistics and analysis are necessary concerning multiple outcomes that will eventually take place each day during a presidency. No one can imagine the amount of constant and consistent effort as well as the demands upon those who support the efforts of the President and his staff.

It is these areas that determine if a president can make sound and relevant decisions regarding his presidency. What needs are important and necessary to his legacy, how he must get the right information at the right time   during the right circumstances and how he will be perceived historically after his presidency ends. These are only a few of the problems that exist as the President works to keep America free.

ABOUT THE AUTHOR

Taeger Gilmighel Mac'Ethe, a native of Chicago, Illinois has traveled to many countries of the world. Taeger enjoys writing, painting, programming and playing guitar. He studied Political Science and Pre-Law at the university and went on to work in public service after graduating. He later spent much of his career in the field of information technology where he continues today.